OXFORD MEDICAL PUBLICATIONS

Health Promotion
Models and Values

Health Promotion
Models and Values

R.S. DOWNIE
MA, BPhil, FRSE
Professor of Moral Philosophy
University of Glasgow

CAROL FYFE
BA, MPH, PhD
Evaluation Manager
Health Promotion Department
Greater Glasgow Health Board

and

ANDREW TANNAHILL
MB, ChB, MSc, MFPHM
Formerly Senior Lecturer in Public Health Medicine
University of Glasgow

Oxford   New York   Tokyo
OXFORD UNIVERSITY PRESS

Oxford University Press, Walton Street, Oxford OX2 6DP

Oxford New York Toronto
Delhi Bombay Calcutta Madras Karachi
Petaling Jaya Singapore Hong Kong Tokyo
Nairobi Dar es Salaam Cape Town
Melbourne Auckland
and associated companies in
Berlin Ibadan

Oxford is a trade mark of Oxford University Press

Published in the United States
by Oxford University Press, New York

British Library Cataloguing in Publication Data
Health promotion.
1. Health education
I. Downie, R. S. (Robert Silcock), 1933–   II. Fyfe, Carol
III. Tannahill, Andrew
613'.07
ISBN 0-19-261739-7 (Pbk)

Library of Congress Cataloguing in Publication Data
Downie, R. S. (Robert Silcock)
Health promotion : models and values / R.S. Downie, Carol Fyfe,
and Andrew Tannahill.
(Oxford medical publications)
Includes bibliographical references.
1. Health promotion. I. Fyfe, Carol. II. Tannahill, Andrew.
III. Title. IV. Series.
RA427.8.D68   1990
362.1'01—dc20   89-23076
ISBN 0-19-261739-7 (Pbk)

Printed in Great Britain by
Biddles Ltd, Guildford and King's Lynn

Foreword

Kenneth Calman
Chief Medical Officer, Scottish Home and Health Department

The preservation and maintenance of health is of paramount importance to everyone. But what do we mean by health, and is it a social
value, or a concept which relates solely to the individual? These questions have been part of our intellectual heritage for centuries, and are
just as relevant today. In this book Professor Downie, Dr Fyfe, and
Dr Tannahill bring together a philosophical and a practical approach
to issues of health and health promotion in order to shed new light on
the ways in which the public health can be improved.

An analysis of what determines health reveals that at least five factors interact to influence the health of an individual or population.
These include *biological factors*, such as ageing and genetic changes;
lifestyle, including behaviour; *environment*, which includes communicable diseases; *social and economic factors*; and *use of and access to
health services*. With each of these factors there is a major role for
health promotion in the improvement of the health of the population,
emphasizing the definition of health arrived at in the book that
'health' is not an absolute concept, but something which can, and
must, be constantly improved. Health targets therefore, such as
lowering mortality rates, increasing uptake of immunization,
changes in lifestyle etc., must not be seen as ends in themselves but as steps on the way to improving health and quality of
life.

The book also emphasizes the fact that health has many dimensions, physical, social, psychological, and that it is not just a 'medical' issue but one which is relevant to all health care professionals,
and the public at large. Part of this book therefore is concerned
with the vocabulary of health promotion and how the words used by
the public, the philosopher, the doctor, the educationalist, and
many others, sometimes require clarification. Moreover, the same
concept is sometimes called by a different name by different
groups. Lifeskills, self-esteem, empowerment, and autonomy

might be examples of such words.

A major part of this book is about evaluation, a key issue in health promotion. The approach taken is to identify the concepts involved and to provide an overview of this critical area. In a similar way the question of values in health and health promotion is tackled sensitively and in a practical way.

Scotland has a long and distinguished tradition of public health, which has always been concerned with the wider determinants of health including social and economic aspects, lifestyle, and the environment. This book, with which I am delighted to be associated, provides an important contribution to this tradition and a framework onto which health promotion projects can be built and evaluated.

There is an old Gaelic saying, 'Is e an oighreachd an t-slainte', which translated means 'Health is the inheritance'. This encapsulates much of the thought behind this book. Health and its promotion are to be seen not only in the short-term but also require to be built into the consciousness of the public and professionals in order that change and improvement can be continually effected. Future generations may judge us by our response to issues relating to health.

Preface

The overall philosophy of traditional health care is largely acceptable to the general public. The same cannot be said for health promotion, partly because it is a relatively new and unfamiliar field, but mainly due to the fact that it confronts many of our comfortable assumptions about health, medicine, lifestyle, and environment. Health promotion challenges us to see both ourselves and our society in a new light, and to alter radically the ways in which we perceive and pursue health. This book is aimed at helping people in a wide range of walks of life to rise to these challenges.

The multidisciplinary nature of health promotion is reflected in the collaboration of the three of us, from very different academic backgrounds, in furthering this aim. We have tried to integrate our various perspectives into a unified philosophy of health promotion, pulling together threads from medicine, education, social sciences, philosophy, and health promotion research and practice.

We hope that the book will be of interest and value to all those who have major contributions to make to health promotion and public health, including students and practitioners in the many branches of medicine and nursing, in health education/promotion, in environmental health, in education, and in social work, as well as politicians, community activists, and members of the public at large.

We are indebted to a number of friends and colleagues. We should like to thank especially Professor Kenneth Calman, who has taken time from his busy schedule as Chief Medical Officer for Scotland to write the Foreword. From his own clinical and teaching experience, and now from the perspective of a Government officer responsible for public health, he is well aware of the complexities of the issues we raise, and he is eminently well-suited to comment on them. We are most grateful to him.

Some of our thoughts on health, values, and justice are built on ideas first introduced in *Caring and Curing* (Downie and Telfer 1980), and we wish to thank Elizabeth Telfer for further discussing them. We also wish to acknowledge gratefully Graham Robertson, whose former close professional relationship with one of us (A.T.) helped with the sowing and germination of conceptual seeds.

Our handwriting and changes of mind have done nothing to enhance the well-being of our secretaries, Anne Valentine and Anne Southall, and we should like to thank them for the patience, diligence, and skill with which they tackled successive drafts of our text.

Glasgow   R.S.D.
April 1989   C.F.
                                                             A.T.

Contents

PART 2: VALUES

Contents   xi

1 Introduction

The term 'health promotion' has come to refer to a movement which gathered momentum in the 1980s. The movement is a radical one which challenges the medicalization of health, stresses its social and economic aspects, and portrays health as having a central place in a flourishing human life. The enthusiasm of those engaged in the movement has led to the development of many ideas on health and how it can be enhanced, but inevitably not all of these ideas are consistent, realistic or well-articulated. This book is concerned with examining and developing out of these ideas workable models of health, its promotion, and its value base.

A whole host of individuals—professional and non-professional —and agencies—statutory and non-statutory—have major contributions to make to health promotion. This book is aimed at helping them towards a greater understanding of the principles of health promotion, an exploration of the underlying philosophy, and a fuller consideration of their actual and potential roles, in partnership with each other and with the communities they serve. We hope that the book will be of value in the preparation and development (formal and personal) of professionals in many fields, including medicine, nursing, other health professions, social work, school and community education, and community development.

The material is presented in two parts. Part 1 embraces key principles of health promotion and offers models for definition, planning, and action. It builds on a broad theoretical base derived from behavioural and educational sciences, epidemiology and clinical practice, and philosophy. This part of the book, although essentially theoretical, is firmly orientated towards practicality, and indeed concludes with a series of examples of principles in practice. To a large extent it represents a distillation of the discussions which constitute Part 2 of the book. The order is intentional: the reader has, through Part 1, easy and immediate access to frameworks for action, and this is backed up by the more detailed account and debate in Part 2.

The central concept of health promotion, and the launching pad of many of its most exciting ideas, is health itself. Accordingly, we begin with an examination of the concept of health, taking as our initial text the much quoted and universally criticized World Health Organization (WHO) definition of health:

Health is a state of complete physical, mental and social well-being, and not merely the absence of disease or infirmity.

This definition makes several important points for our purposes.

First of all, it involves a distinction between health negatively defined—as the absence of ill-health—and health as a positive state—seen as the presence of well-being. Developing this distinction, we assign a substantial amount of our next chapter to the delineation of the negative and positive dimensions of health, and their complex interrelationships. We broaden out from the WHO conception of positive health to include fitness in addition to well-being.

Secondly, the WHO definition includes mental and social as well as physical aspects of health. We acknowledge the importance of these neglected areas, giving some attention to the mental aspects in Chapter 2, and a much larger treatment to the social in Part 2. The unified and enlarged concept of health we argue to be rooted in, and an expression of, the more general idea of the good or flourishing life for human beings. We elaborate this position in our account of fundamental human values in Part 2.

Some of the many uncertainties generated by the health promotion movement concern its relationship to longer established interests of health professionals—health education and public health. Two chapters are therefore given over to advancing models of health education and health promotion, concluding with a brief consideration of their relation to public health. Out of this discussion emerges our recommended definition of health promotion:

Health promotion comprises efforts to enhance positive health and prevent ill-health, through the overlapping spheres of health education, prevention, and health protection.

Some have seen in health promotion ways of cutting costs in traditional health care. But this raises many questions. How do we know whether a health promotion initiative has been effective? Is it just a matter of saving money? Is it mainly to do with increasing people's knowledge of health and its determinants? In a chapter on evaluation we try to show that these and related questions are more complex than they at first seem. In the end, we conclude that health promotion is justifiable on its aims alone, rather than depending on economic arguments.

In dealing with values we note in several contexts that they can be described in different ways, and that new terminology is sometimes introduced for ideas which are familiar in traditional terminology. This is inevitable, in that health promotion is an eclectic discipline and its practitioners come to it from a variety of backgrounds with their own terminologies. For example, health promotion stresses the importance of acquiring 'lifeskills'; but this is just new nomenclature for what, in the philosophy of education, has been called 'self-development'. Again, 'self-esteem' has taken the place of the more traditional 'self-respect'.

We ask our readers to consider how far the concepts of their own disciplines, or of ordinary vocabulary, can be exchanged with or translated into the concepts of health promotion. For instance, medical, nursing, social work, and other health care professionals will be familiar with the concept of 'autonomy' (itself drawn from eighteenth century philosophy). The health promotion movement stresses the importance of what it calls 'empowerment'. But the concept of empowerment simply serves to bring out the fact that many people, whether because of poor health, inadequate housing, unemployment, or low self-esteem, do not have autonomy, or the ability adequately to make choices and determine their own lives. People must therefore be enabled and encouraged to develop autonomy—they must, in a word, be 'empowered'.

One of the key concepts for health promotion is that of an attitude. The concept of an attitude is central because it brings together beliefs, emotions, and behaviour. We therefore devote a chapter to analysing what it means to hold an attitude, and another chapter to suggesting ways in which attitudes can be changed; for the bringing about of changes in attitudes, and consequently in lifestyle, is one of the objectives of health promotion.

It is because it attempts to bring about changes in attitudes and lifestyle that health promotion raises profound questions of moral values. It is therefore necessary to discuss valuing and values. We suggest that the realization of certain values is necessary for the flourishing of human society and human personality. Health itself is a central concept here, for it is one of the values which is not only an essential *means to* human flourishing, but is itself an *expression of* human flourishing. Health is like education in that it is both an 'enabling' good—good for what it brings—and also good in itself, or worthwhile for its own sake.

The majority of writings on health promotion acknowledge the importance of values and the ethical problems of health promotion, but they assign only a small place to the detailed analysis of values and valuing. We try to supplement these writings by bringing out the modifications which health promotion is committed to making in our liberal-democratic tradition—away from an individualistic interpretation of that tradition and back to one based on citizenship.

In view of its commitment to change in individual and social values, health promotion is a politically sensitive activity. For example, it cannot be denied that important determinants of health are the material and social environments. Poor housing, poor education, polluted atmosphere, and unemployment are all factors affecting health, and are all factors with a high political profile. It is therefore impossible to discuss health promotion without being seen as adopting a political stance. We stress that the principles of health promotion will inevitably have political implications, but that it is important to build practice and arguments for change on the solid foundations of these basic principles, rather than resorting to the shorthand vocabulary of politics.

Health care professionals of all kinds, including those involved in health education and health promotion, tend to be practical people who are to an extent suspicious of theory. There is sometimes a contrast implied in health promotion literature between theory, depicted as 'airy-fairy', and practice, depicted as 'down-to-earth'. But we do not necessarily know where we are going or what we are doing just because we claim to be 'down-to-earth'. There is a well-known saying which warns us against not being able to see the wood for the trees! To know where we are going, to have a clear view of the wood, it can be helpful to make an occasional aerial survey. In other words, we must have a good grasp of a philosophy of health promotion, its principles and justification, or we shall be lost in a morass of empirical detail and tips for day-to-day business. Our book is an attempt to state this philosophy explicitly.

There are other reasons for having a clear philosophy of health promotion. The general public and the traditional health care professions can be sceptical of the activities of health promotion, suggesting that anything worthwhile in the movement is done by traditional medicine anyway, and that the rest is just gratuitous interference with lifestyle. It is thus important for those involved with health promotion to be clear on their answers to the questions: 'What is health promotion *for*?'; 'What is distinctive about it?'; and 'Why is it worthwhile?' We therefore hope that our book will provide:

(1) a *bird's eye view of the nature* of health promotion;

(2) an account of its *links* with related health care activities;

(3) a *justification* for it and what it is attempting to do;

(4) an *underlying support* or *value base* for its practical activities.

In the film *Educating Rita*, Rita, having begun her education, goes back to the pub with her parents and listens to the singing. She is dissatisfied with it and says: 'There must be better tunes'. Health promotion seems to us to be committed to the belief that indeed there are better tunes—better and worse lifestyles. This is not to say that there is only one good way to live, but unless we are convinced that some lifestyles are better than others for helping human nature to flourish we can see no point in health promotion.

Part 1 Models

2 Health

The growth of interest and activity in health promotion in recent times has been accompanied by many attempts to delineate health itself. This is understandable: it may be reasonably argued that, just as a history or chemistry teacher needs to know his or her subject in order to teach it, so must a 'health promoter' have a clear idea of what it is that is to be promoted.

Attempts at delineating health have been directed along two lines: the pursuit of a neat definition, and the description of a number of 'models' of health. Neither set of efforts has been entirely successful. In the first place, the simple intuitive notions which we all have about our own (and others') health have proved not to be readily translatable into a brief but adequate definition. Secondly, models —'biomedical', 'social', 'welfare', and the like—have been falsely presented as distinct aspects or views of health in watertight compartments, with consequent neglect of how the various components are integrated.

In this chapter, we explore the meaning of health and construct a model which seeks to pull together the many and varied strands that together constitute health. This enables us to identify an overall goal for health promotion.

2.1 Defining health

The most commonly quoted definition of health, as noted in our introductory chapter, is that presented in the Constitution of the World Health Organization (WHO 1946):

Health is a state of complete physical, mental and social well-being, and not merely the absence of disease or infirmity.

This definition has been widely criticized. However, as we shall show, there are merits along with the shortcomings. In the first instance we shall concentrate on only one aspect of the definition, namely the distinction between negative and positive aspects of health.

The former is negative in two respects: health is viewed (in a negative sense) as involving the *absence* of disease or infirmity (themselves *negative* in connotation). Similarly, the latter is positive in two ways: health is seen (positively) as entailing the *presence* of a (*positive*) quality—well-being.

No matter how often the WHO definition or similar constructs are cited by health professionals (among others), it is true to say that in practice the positive aspect of health tends to be neglected. It is a well-worn, but nonetheless true, cliché that we have a National *Sickness* Service rather than a National Health Service. Even with the rise of health promotion, attention has been skewed towards the prevention of ill-health as opposed to the promotion of the positive dimension.

2.2 Negative health

The familiar, and currently dominant, negative dimension of health—which we shall refer to as *ill-health*—is not as straightforward as may be assumed. In speaking about ill-health, one might be referring to disease, injury, illness, disability or handicap, singly or in various combinations and experienced over a long or a short period of time.

Disease and illness are not synonymous. Someone may feel, and be seen to be, ill as a result of a diagnosed disease. Someone else, on the other hand, may have a disease without any illness manifestation, for example a skin condition presenting only as a rash, or even a presymptomatic cancer. Equally, another person may feel or look ill in the absence of a disease or injury: he or she may be situationally depressed, or have taken an overdose, or simply have a hangover. Clearly, to describe ill-health in terms either of disease or of illness would be incomplete without mention of the other; we shall therefore have to give an account of ill-health in terms of both notions. Let us explore their meaning and relationship further.

2.2.1 Disease and illness as disorders

Illness is a less technical notion than disease. Any lay person, including the sufferer, can know that someone is ill without knowing whether or not he or she has a disease, let alone what disease it is. At least this is true of physical illness; mental illness, as we shall see, may be more difficult. Taking physical illness only for the time being, let us consider what makes someone say that he or she (or another person) is ill. Relevant factors are what many would call overall upsets of the system: for example, not wanting to eat, feeling and being weak, feeling abnormally hot or cold, or having a weak pulse. People who are ill will often have headaches or rashes or itches, but these isolated phenomena would not in themselves constitute being ill. Thus someone can say: 'When I had German measles I came out in a splendid rash but I wasn't ill at all', meaning that he or she was not (or not very) feverish, ate normally, felt strong, etc. Again, people who have a stye or boil are not ill simply thereby, although if they get a fever as a result of this kind of infection, they are then said to be ill.

So far we have made no distinction between *being* ill and *feeling* ill. The sense of this distinction is far from clear. One distinction might be between the symptoms of which only the sufferer is aware—aches and pains, feelings of faintness or nausea—and the signs which can be detected by others, such as raised temperature or quickened pulse. If a patient reports a series of untoward feelings but the doctor can 'find nothing' he or she might say, 'You aren't really ill.' Similarly, persons with German measles who have a rash but feel fine, instead of saying 'I'm not ill' might equally well say 'I don't *feel* ill', implying that since they have German measles they *are* in fact ill.

But this distinction between the objective conditions and the subjective ones is not an exhaustive account of the difference between being ill and feeling ill. For, if people go on reporting headaches, giddiness, and so on of sufficient severity, and we believe them, we might well say not just that they *feel* ill, but that they *are* ill with some as yet mysterious condition. Of course, many a doctor in such a case may say (or at any rate think): 'You're not really ill, it's just your nerves.' But then the same view could be expressed, perhaps more charitably, by saying 'It's your nerves which are making you ill.' The distinction between being and feeling ill, then, is sometimes between the objective and the subjective, sometimes between the temporary and persistent, and sometimes between the mental and the physical.

Disease is a more technical notion than illness, as we said earlier. A person who has a disease suffers from some medically defined condition which is identifiable as similar to that suffered from by some others.

A crucial notion in both illness and disease is that of *upset* or *disorder*. We can partly understand this if we think of the human body as a machine, in which various processes (such as digestion and excretion, maintenance of a certain temperature, inhaling of oxygen) necessary to its maintenance and smooth working are carried out, and through which the person whose body it is carries out his or her actions. On this model an upset or disorder would be some failure in the system which prevented the machine working properly, and what was wrong or bad about it would be precisely this interference with the machine's normal working.

2.2.2 Disease and illness as unwanted states

The above mechanistic model of ill-health is only partly satisfactory. For one thing, it does not accommodate pain and other subjective symptoms, such as nausea, feeling faint, etc. It might be retorted that this is in the nature of the case, since pain and other feelings are essentially inward and non-mechanistic. In any case, it might be said, they are indicators of the disorder rather than parts of it and so their analogue in mechanical terms would be with the untoward sounds with which motorists become obsessed. But this will not quite do either. There can be pain with no apparent organic cause, and in a case like this we would not say: 'Since the mechanism is working normally that's all that matters.' The pain itself constitutes a disorder which must be put right. No doubt if severe it will psychologically interfere with the sufferer's activities, but even where it does not, the presence of pain is still in itself a matter for medical attention, and a person in pain, even from no apparent cause, is regarded as ill or at any rate not well.

So far, then, we have two kinds of phenomena that constitute ill-health: what may be termed mechanical failure, and some other discomfort. Is there any way of linking these two factors? One possible line which suggests itself is that both pain and malfunction are *unpleasant* things for those who have them. This assertion would, of course, need a little qualification. Some pain, in some circumstances, can be pleasant, and illness can be positively welcome—if for example it gets one out of the Army. But in general terms pain is unpleasant, and, in general, being incapacitated prevents people from doing whatever they want to do—at least as regards normal plans and projects. Can we then say that the disorder which characterizes illness and disease, and which takes the form both of discomfort and of mechanical failure, is to be described as a (physical) condition which is in general unpleasant or prevents people from doing what they want?

2.2.3 Disease and illness as abnormal states

This will not do, for there are examples of such conditions which are clearly not illnesses, for instance the weakness and loss of faculties that accompany ageing. These are not regarded as illnesses because they are 'natural' or 'normal'. In other words, everyone goes through something of the kind, or at any rate suffers some out of a range of unpleasant changes. There is therefore an idea of the *normal* against which certain kinds of change are judged to be illnesses, others not. In a similar way, the pains of childbirth, arising as they do from a natural process, are regarded as normal, rather as aching muscles after strenuous or unaccustomed exercise are regarded as normal.

We can say, then, that a condition is to be regarded as a disorder, and not merely as unpleasant, by reference to a conception of a normal state for human beings. The aspect of abnormality is indeed uppermost in some cases of disease. As we said earlier, minor skin diseases may not make a person ill in any way or cause any discomfort, and what makes them *diseases* is that they constitute abnormal conditions of the skin. Of course, they are as a rule undesirable to their possessor, because they are unsightly, but the verdict of unsightliness is largely dependent on the judgement of abnormality.

2.2.4 Disabilities, deformities, and unwanted states

At this point it may well be objected that to distinguish normal from abnormal changes and call only the latter illnesses and diseases is totally artificial, as doctors and others are also concerned with trying to arrest normal changes if they are undesirable; for example, to lessen the effects of ageing with appropriate diet and exercise, or hormone therapy. It is important to note, however, that if young children have stiff joints we might say there is something wrong with them, whereas if old people have stiff joints we might say that they are not as agile as they were. There is a difference not only in how the two situations are described, but also in how they are dealt with. No doubt doctors do try to alleviate such concomitants of old age but, if the two disabilities were equal, there would be much more doubt about spending a lot of effort on such activity than there would be in the case of the child because there is an idea that older people 'shouldn't expect' to be as mobile as they were.

A parallel situation occurs with regard to deformity and less obvious cosmetic problems. Certainly, doctors do regard it as part of their business to correct abnormalities of appearance (with plastic surgery) if they are extreme, but if they are mild they do not seem to make the automatic claim for aid that a deformity such as harelip does. Similarly, they will regard it as their business to alleviate the pains of childbirth if required to do so, but there is no expectation that all trace of discomfort will be relieved. In our conception of disease and illness, then, there is a built-in implication of some normal condition of the human body by reference to which these things are aberrations.

2.2.5 Disease and illness as 'law-like'

We have said that deformity is analogous to illness in being a disorder which medicine is concerned to treat—or better still, of course, to prevent. But it should be noticed that deformity, unlike some illness and disease, is not as such incompatible with good health. Of course, there are some deformities, such as 'holes in the heart', which produce mechanical failures, and a sufferer from these is said to be in poor health. But a child who is born deaf is not merely by dint of this defect called unhealthy. It is true that a person who is severely handicapped in this way might hesitate before stating on a form that he or she is in good health, but broadly speaking these handicaps, severe though they are, are somehow not thought of as impairing *health*. This is difficult to understand in terms of our account so far, which depicts ill-health as uncomfortable or frustrating abnormalities of a system.

The explanation seems to be that illness and disease are seen as things which essentially progress or change in a law-like manner, which have a life of their own. In such cases one can always sensibly ask whether the sufferer is getting better or worse. Being ill is essentially an unstable situation. The deaf child, by contrast, is fixed in disability, and so not regarded as unhealthy because there is nothing untoward going on in him or her. But the fact, if it is one, that the deformed person is not regarded as unhealthy does not mean that doctors or others have no concern with trying to prevent such cases or to alleviate their lot—with false limbs, plastic surgery, etc. What it means, rather, is that health, in the negative sense, is too narrow to be regarded as the goal of health care. What we need instead is some notion of positive health or physical 'wholeness' which includes not

only what is implied by the absence of ill-health but additional
elements. We shall pick up on this notion in due course.

2.2.6 Injury

It should be noted that some of the points which apply to deformity
apply also to *injury*. Sometimes people who have been badly injured
are described as ill, and when this is so they are suffering from the
same kinds of incapacity that attend other illness—weakness, faintness, unconsciousness, etc. But if the lack of capacity is simply the
essential result of the injury, then the sufferer might in one sense be
in good health. A skier who has broken a leg cannot walk, but may
be in glowing health. The doctor's task here may again be described
as the restoration not of health but of wholeness. But injury is in one
respect more like illness than deformity: it can progress in that it can
heal.

We can summarize this account of physical ill-health by saying that
it can occur in episodes or over long periods, that it can manifest itself
in illness, disease, deformity, or injury, and that these overlapping
concepts can be linked if they are seen on the model of *abnormal*,
unwanted, or *incapacitating* states of a biological system.

2.2.7 Mental and social ill-health

So far we have focused on *physical* ill-health, as happens all too
often in discussions of health and in health service planning and
practice. The situation becomes even more complex when we remind
ourselves of the existence of the very important mental and social
facets. Important concepts touched on above as part of physical
ill-health—disease, injury, illness, disability, and handicap—may
be applied, albeit with varying readiness, to both of these additional
elements of health.

We summarized our views of physical ill-health by saying that it
consists of the presence of physically *abnormal conditions* (such as
diseases or deformities) and/or *unwanted conditions* (such as skin
rashes) and/or *incapacitating conditions* (such as injuries to limbs).
Let us try to carry these ideas over to the sphere of the mental and
social. Take first abnormality.

The idea of abnormal or sick states of mind is much less obvious
and a source of much more disagreement than that of abnormal
bodily states. The reason for this is that in the case of the body the

'abnormal' is specified in terms of an objective biological norm, whereas in the case of the mind the norm is a culturally relative, social or statistical norm. Moreover, the further suggestion that anyone who has an abnormal state of mind is mentally ill is at the beginning of a path which leads to the conclusion that 'immorality', or even the non-conformity of minority social groups, as examples of 'deviance', are forms of mental illness. To construe any 'deviant' behaviour as being necessarily the product of 'sick' or 'abnormal' desires and therefore a sign of mental illness is to give a spurious air of objectivity to what is largely culture-relative, and it may also be to deny responsibility for action to those regarded as social wrongdoers. It is down this road that we encounter the Soviet psychiatrists who used to treat as mentally ill those who criticized the regime.

Confusion over the idea of abnormal states of mind is due to the fact that three different concepts are being run together—sick desires, minority desires, and immoral or illegal desires. It is not easy to draw satisfying distinctions between these concepts, but we might say that a 'sick' desire is one which people cannot make sense of in terms of their own experience, and which is destructive of human personality. A minority or eccentric desire is one which (statistically) is not common, but it may or may not be 'sick', 'immoral' or 'illegal'—for example, a desire to collect old typewriters. An immoral or illegal desire is harmful to the person concerned or to society generally, but it may or may not be sick and it may or may not be minority. For example, a desire to steal one's neighbour's property is (perhaps) a minority desire, it is immoral (and illegal if implemented), but it is not sick. But a desire to collect nail clippings from corpses is sick, because it bears no relation to any of the reasons for which people collect things, and it is obviously a minority desire; but it is not as such immoral since it causes no harm. This way of drawing the line between the three classes of desire, all called 'abnormal', is only rough and ready, but scientific precision cannot be expected. Nevertheless, the distinctions are important.

The second idea of mental illness, as an unwanted state, is also difficult. In the case of physical illness it is the sufferers themselves who do not want the condition in which they find themselves. But in the case of mental illness what is wrong, sometimes at least, is that sufferers are content with the state they are in. Of course, the fact that someone has sick desires in itself gives no warrant for interfering with him or her. The psychopath, on the other hand, is harming others—other people suffer from the state more directly than he or she—and one thing wrong with the psychopath is precisely that he or she is not disturbed by the sick wants and does not request that they be treated. Hence, whereas some of those who are mentally ill may want to be rid of their states, this is by no means characteristic and there are therefore uncertainties in the carry-over of the idea of unwanted states from physical to mental ill-health.

To try to avoid the difficulties in the idea of unwanted states we can turn to the third strand in the concept of ill-health—that of loss of capacity. According to this account, just as physical disease means that the body cannot fulfil its function, so mental disease means that people cannot do what they are normally able to do in the mental sphere—reason, understand their world, or exercise their will. On this account, typical cases of mental illness are obsessive—compulsive neurosis (showing itself, for example, in repetitive actions which the patient cannot help doing), or incapacitating depression. But it would follow that psychopathy, showing itself not in loss of capacity but in frightful behaviour which the agent wilfully carries out, is not a mental illness at all. That conclusion is counter-intuitive, and hence we need all three accounts of mental ill-health, as with physical ill-health—in terms of abnormal states, unwanted states, and incapaciting states.

2.2.8 Summary

The physical, mental and social *facets* of ill-health are inextricably interlinked: serious or troublesome physical illness, for example, may lead to mental ill-health (a depressive or anxiety state, perhaps) or social impairment; likewise mental illness may result in physical ill-health (such as injury arising from failed suicide) or social handicap. Similarly, physical, mental, and social *factors*—determinants of ill-health—may respectively damage other aspects of health: for instance, low socio-economic status is associated with a wide range of physical and mental health problems.

Given the complexity of ill-health—with its physical, mental, and social facets and determinants, and its subjective and objective aspects—a person's level of ill-health is clearly far less straightforward to assess fully than is perhaps implied from the day-to-day work of doctors and other health professionals.

2.3 Well-being

We shall now move on to consider the positive dimension of health as embraced by the WHO definition—well-being. Let us begin by attempting to provide an analysis of a complex concept.

We shall look first at *feelings* of well-being. 'Well-being' some-times means no more than people's subjective estimations of mood or level of happiness on a given occasion. In this sense, they them-selves are the only authority on their well-being, and there is no implication as to how they have come to be in that state or how long it will last. If they are 'feeling great' then they have a high degree of subjective well-being whether that state will last minutes or a life-time, whether it is brought about by being in love, going for a swim, good weather, or alcohol.

Subjective well-being, however, may be spurious. It may arise from influences which are overall detrimental to an individual's functioning or flourishing, and/or to society. In other words, as with ill-health, we must look to a more objective assessment of well-being. In doing so it is important to pay attention to the *origins* of feelings of well-being.

To take a crude example, the notion of the enhancement of well-being as a pre-eminent goal of health promotion has been ques-tioned by some who would suggest that this goal could be achieved by the mass administration of heroin to the population. One could not reasonably argue that narcotic-induced euphoria constitutes a state of positive health. Similarly, it would be difficult to make a case for viewing an acute schizophrenic state with mood elevation and a blissful lack of insight as one of positive health. Subjective well-being, then, must stand up to some sort of outside scrutiny if we are to consider it to be a true state of well-being—reflecting positive health. As part of this scrutiny we must look critically at the *basis* of feelings of well-being. We argue that *true* well-being involves and reflects a quality which we shall refer to as *empowerment*, and which we examine below.

This concept of true well-being is much more structured than that of subjective well-being, and contains essential reference to some conception of the 'good life' for a human being. A great deal of wisdom has been accumulated over the centuries about the kinds of activities which make for a flourishing human life. Important here will be some conception of having a measure of control over one's life, of being able to choose what one wants to do or be, and of being able to develop one's talents. This strand in the idea of well-being has a social and political side to it as well. Experience teaches that, on the whole, most people have a much more lasting and deeper level of well-being (or happiness) if they have friends, if they have some confidence that their material needs are going to be satisfied, if they are not going to be put in prison in an arbitrary way, and so on. We shall say much more about this strand to well-being in Chapters 9–11, where we shall connect it with the more traditional concept of autonomy and the newer expression of autonomy in the idea of empowerment.

Subjective (or hedonistic) well-being, then, can exist with or without true ('good life') well-being. It *can* be brought about by acquiring lifeskills and achieving autonomy or empowerment. This point is of the first importance for health promotion and indeed for health care more generally. Let us take an example. Imagine a single parent who consults her general practitioner (GP) because she feels depressed. The temptation for the GP may well be to prescribe an anxiolytic drug which will make the patient feel better about herself and her situation. In other words, the GP can induce a state of subjective well-being. The disadvantage of this approach is that the well-being depends on the continuing use of the drug. On the other hand, the approach of a health educationist might be to encourage the single parent to be in touch with others in similar situations and to get all the financial and other support to which she is legally entitled. In other words, the second approach is directed towards the acquisition or development of lifeskills and autonomy, or empowerment.

This second approach to the promotion of well-being is slower, but it is the only one which in the long term will achieve a lasting, true well-being. To say this is not, of course, to suggest that there may not be contexts for short-term remedies, or to underestimate the problems in the second method. We shall discuss in more detail the concepts of the objectivist, 'good life' approach to well-being in later chapters (see especially Chapter 9). In the meantime it is sufficient to note that the biomedical approach to health tends to involve the subjective sense of well-being since it can be drug-induced, whereas the health promotion approach, with its stress on 'being all you can be', must assume the second, 'good life' sense.

2.4 Linking well-being and ill-health

Let us now turn to look at the connection between well-being and ill-health. Attempts to relate the two concepts or similar ideas have generally taken the form of a continuum (Catford 1983), with extremes of well-being and ill-health at the positive and negative ends, respectively (Fig. 2.1).

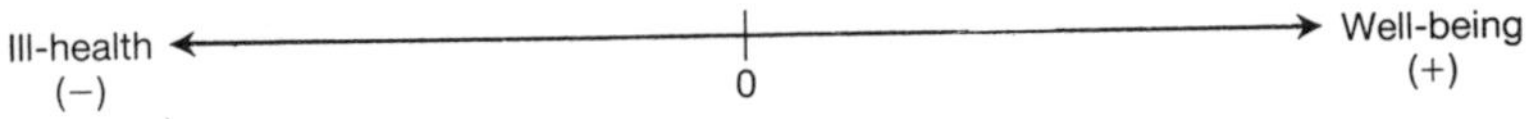

Ill-health ◄————————————————|————————————————► Well-being
(−)   0   (+)

Fig 2.1   Health as a continuum.

Even leaving aside objections (religious and otherwise) to the tendency to present death as the ultimate in ill-health rather than an ultimate consequence of it, this sort of schema is unsatisfactory. It is possible to feel full of well-being in the presence of serious or even life-threatening disease; equally one may be free of illness, with the benefit of medical evidence, without enjoying a feeling of well-being. It thus makes more sense to present well-being and ill-health as two axes at right angles to, and crossing, each other (Fig. 2.2).

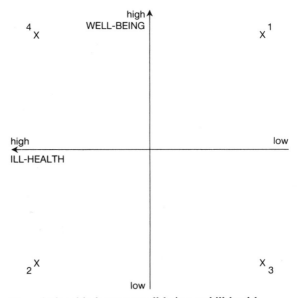

Fig 2.2   The relationship between well-being and ill-health.

Since ill-health is a negative entity, the horizontal axis is presented, somewhat unusually, as having 'high' to the left and 'low' to the right. This has the effect of preserving the mathematical convention of positive x and y co-ordinates in the right upper quadrant, making for easier conceptualization.

We shall now consider four individuals (numbered 1 to 4) plotted on Fig. 2.2 according to characteristics of (true) well-being and ill-health at a given point in time.

1. This individual is free of ill-health, and this is matched by a high level of well-being. This is clearly a highly desirable state.

2. This person has a high level of ill-health and a correspondingly low level of well-being. He or she may, for example, have terminal cancer, be in a great deal of pain, and feel desolate.

3. The third individual does not feel ill, and has no other evidence of ill-health, but for some reason this state is accompanied by a low level of well-being. He or she may, for instance, feel too socially unskilled or physically unfit to enjoy a 'clean bill of health'.

4. This person is experiencing a high level of well-being despite a high level of ill-health. Such people may feel in peak physical condition, unaware of an advanced malignancy, or may be terminally ill but well-adjusted to their fate, at peace with themselves and the world.

The reader may have noticed the physical, mental, and social facets of well-being alluded to above, consistent with the WHO view of health. As is the case with negative health, levels of well-being according to the three sets of criteria may be similar or different at any time. Also, like ill-health, aspects of well-being may be short-lived (especially in the case of purely subjective well-being) or longer term.

2.5 Fitness

Another quality commonly arises in discussion of *positive health*, namely *fitness*. Consideration of this characteristically focuses on *physical* attributes, commonly 'the Four S's': Strength, Stamina, Suppleness, and Skills. We shall therefore start on familiar territory, by considering physical fitness as an element of positive health.

Criteria for assessing physical fitness form a spectrum in which we can distinguish three main points. At one end of this spectrum, fitness is viewed simply as the ability to execute ordinary, everyday tasks without undue physical discomfort (such as muscle aches). It is assessed in relation to targets arising from a person's normal daily life, and according to the presence, absence, or degree of physical consequences of carrying out routine activities. Individuals have their own personal indicators of physical fitness, integral to their life situation—such as being able to run for a bus, or carry a child or a load of bricks. As long as people manage to attain their own targets with regard to their particular set of indicators, they may regard themselves as fit, according to this minimalist view of physical fitness. Personal indicators and targets will, naturally, vary throughout someone's life, in relation to age, disability, etc.

Moving along the spectrum of functioning to a second point, we may adopt a more refined view of physical fitness by seeing it in terms of suitability to perform highly specialized roles or tasks. For example, someone may be considered, on the basis of certain criteria, to be fit to be a dancer in a particular *corps de ballet*, or a player in a given football team. Particular aspects of physical fitness need to be developed to a given degree for a special purpose. As with the minimalist view, fitness is seen as a means to an end.

At the opposite end of the spectrum from the minimalist view we have a third idea, that of maximizing the efficiency and effectiveness of the body as a machine: developing the capacity of the heart as a pump, of the lungs as gas exchangers, and of body muscles as sources of power. Efforts to maximize physical fitness may be a means to an end: training may be aimed at one's capabilities in a specific role (such as sprinting or dancing), and fitness will then be gauged according to performance in that role. This is not always the case, however. People may seek to develop physical fitness as an end in itself: tests of fitness may become relegated to a series of gymnasium tests and visual assessment of muscle bulk; pursuit of fitness may become an obsession, divorced from the basic requirements for a balanced and fruitful life.

It is easy to see that physical fitness will often be accompanied by feelings of well-being. Indeed, true physical fitness (as distinct from spurious feelings which could not stand up to some sort of test) might reasonably be seen as the physical counterpart of the essentially mental and social qualities of empowerment referred to in Section 2.3. Furthermore, one might even argue that the concept of a functional spectrum of physical fitness—from *minimalist* through *specialist* to *maximalist*—is also applicable to mental and social considerations. Such explorations lead us rapidly into murky waters, however, and so we shall move on without further discussion to a relatively simple, but nonetheless useful, delineation of positive health.

2.6 Positive health

We see positive health as comprising true well-being (with its roots in empowerment, and of considerable value to the individual and society) together with the related notion of fitness, and as having physical, mental, and social ingredients. We shall go no further towards attempting to tease out these threads.

We consider that a state of positive health involves high levels of both components, true well-being and fitness. Moreover, such a state entails an appropriate *balance* of the physical, mental, and social ingredients: over-concentration on one may be to the detriment of either or both of the others. For example, an extreme commitment to physical training may interfere with the development or maintenance of mental or social skills, and may militate against mental and social well-being.

2.7 A model of health

We shall now examine how a model of health may be synthesized from the complex and interrelated ingredients which we have identified in this chapter, with a view to elucidating an overall goal for health promotion.

First we shall return to the WHO definition of health. We wholeheartedly approve of the way in which this definition alerts one to the inextricably interlinked physical, mental, and social facets of health, and to its positive and negative dimensions. However, we have drawn attention to the inadequacy of regarding *all* well-being as indicative of positive health (recall the distinction between spurious and true well-being). Furthermore, we have raised the concept of fitness as part of positive health. Moreover, we join with others before us in criticizing the Utopian nature of the construct in describing a 'complete state'. Finally, we suggest that the definition is misleading in implying that health is an *absolute* concept. Rather, we see health as *relative*: health promotion must help people to *better* health rather than seeking to attain a specified *level* of health.

The model shown as Fig. 2.3 is an attempt to summarize the elements of health and their interrelationships.

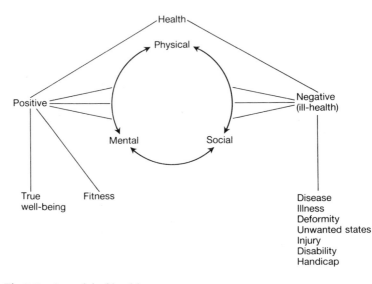

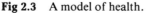

Fig 2.3   A model of health.

Both positive and negative health are to be seen as having interconnected physical, mental, and social elements. The representation of these facets as bridges between positive and negative reminds us that levels of positive health and ill-health in relation to one particular facet often go hand in hand; physical illness may well be accompanied by a low level of physical well-being or fitness, for instance. We should, however, remember from the earlier account that well-being is not always inversely related to ill-health; neither is fitness invariably thus related to ill-health—someone may have cancer but be fit, for example. Indeed, we can represent the relationship between positive health—comprising true well-being and fitness—and ill-health by substituting 'positive health' for 'well-being' in Fig. 2.2.

Health has to be seen as the sum or product of all its components, and, if we bear in mind the complexity of the many points we have made in this chapter, we see that the *precise* quantification of an individual's health is impossible. When we speak of 'improving health' we must be referring to increasing the overall 'quantity' of health, by enhancing positive health, reducing negative health, or both. It may clearly be very difficult to judge whether an increase of this sort, whether at the level of the individual or on a population scale, has indeed taken place as a result of intervention, given the unpredictable relationship between positive and negative health, and the interconnections between physical, mental, and social facets. The final decision is likely to be based on value judgements—on whether the positive dimension is given precedence over the negative, on the relative importance attached to physical, mental, and social criteria, and so on. Self-perceived health may thus differ significantly from others-perceived, not just because of the presence of 'untestable' subjective elements of health as described earlier, but also as a result of differing value systems. The issue of measuring health is discussed more fully in Chapter 5.

2.8 The goal of health promotion

The lack of a clear-cut, predictable association between negative and positive health has implications for the goal of health promotion. Health promotion must seek to prevent ill-health in such a way as simultaneously to enhance positive health: blinkered attention to prevention might result in behaviour geared so much to risk avoidance that positive health—both well-being and fitness—would suffer. Health promotion must also attempt to develop positive health with an eye on prevention: for example, encouragement to take physical exercise, through cycling or running, perhaps, should take into account the risks of injury, and should build in appropriate safety measures.

The *overall goal* of health promotion may be summed up as *the balanced enhancement of physical, mental, and social facets of positive health, coupled with the prevention of physical, mental and social ill-health.*

The reader should not be discouraged from developing his or her role in health promotion as a result of the breadth of scope of this goal. While we should certainly encourage everyone to consider carefully the full range of his or her potential contributions, we freely admit that the individual is unlikely to be in a position to contribute greatly towards all the various components of the goal. Indeed, the pressing message is that a great many individuals and agencies have parts to play in health promotion, and should work together towards achieving its overall goal.

2.9 Conclusions

1. The WHO definition of health distinguishes a positive and a negative dimension to health.

2. Negative health, or ill-health, has a subjective component expressed in the concepts of illness and discomfort, and an objective component expressed in concepts of disease, injury, handicap, or deformity. These strands are linked via the idea of abnormal, unwanted or incapacitating states of a biological system, which in turn presupposes the idea of a good or flourishing human life.

3. These ideas can be carried over to the spheres of the mental and social.

4. Positive health has two components: well-being and fitness.

5. Well-being can be purely subjective, but to be a component of positive health it must arise from and reflect a process of empowerment, which may be enhanced through the development of lifeskills.

6. Fitness can be seen on a spectrum from minimalist through functionalist to maximalist.

7. The overall goal of health promotion is the balanced enhancement of physical, mental, and social positive health, coupled with the prevention of physical, mental, and social ill-health.

8. A great many individuals and agencies may work together towards this goal.

3 Health education

In this chapter, principles of health education are examined in detail. This is essential before attempting to place this long-established field of activity within the context of the broader and newer concept of health promotion (see Chapter 4).

People have firm, and varied, views regarding the nature of health education. Interpretations are influenced by professional background and experience and, among other factors, by perceptions of the meanings of the component words, 'health' and 'education'. Too often health education is perceived by powerful individuals and groups (such as politicians and doctors), as being essentially a simple matter of telling people what they ought to do to be healthy. Dangerous oversimplifications of this sort among key potential health educators have gone hand in hand with a tendency for health education to be treated as an 'instant expert' subject. This chapter is aimed primarily at helping the vast and varied legions of health educators to a common understanding of the principles and scope of health education.

3.1 Definitions

Many definitions of health education have been offered in recent years. We shall consider only two.

Smith's (1979) definition suggests that we all receive 'health education' of various sorts as we simply go through the business of living:

In the widest sense, health education may be defined as the sum total of all influences that collectively determine knowledge, belief and behaviour related to the promotion, maintenance and restoration of health in individuals and communities. These influences comprise formal and informal education in the family, in the school and in society at large, as well as in the special context of health service activities.

Although many would dispute this use of the term 'education' to cover such a wide range of learning experience (incidental as well as

27

intentional), this exposition is valuable in a number of ways. It points to the wide range of settings and circumstances in which influences on health may be exerted. It touches on the collective dimension of health (a community is, of course, more than just the sum of its individuals, and one person's actions may affect another's health; see Chapters 10 and 11). Furthermore, it embraces influences which are exerted without any health-related intent (which may be health enhancing or health damaging). Last, it brings to mind important, deliberately imposed influences which are not aimed at health enhancement: some are dressed up as being pro-health, but are in truth aimed at the promotion of something else (some materials produced by the dairy industry are an example); others concern the purposeful promotion of products, etc., which are patently damaging (tobacco advertising, for instance). Mike Daube (formerly Senior Lecturer in Health Education, University of Edinburgh) has referred to such efforts as '*pseudo-health education*' and '*anti-health education*', respectively.

Smith's broad interpretation thus serves as an important reminder of the background which must be recognized and addressed by the wide range of people who are concerned with the promotion of health through education. Clearly, however, it is purposefully provided pro-health education that is the main concern of this book, and henceforth the term 'health education' will be used purely in this context. We may define this important subset of Smith's definition as follows:

Health education is communication activity aimed at enhancing positive health and preventing or diminishing ill-health in individuals and groups, through influencing the beliefs, attitudes, and behaviour of those with power and of the community at large.

Note the reference to power-holders in society. These include politicians, industrialists and other businessmen, and professionals within and outside the health service. This recognition that responsibilities in relation to health do not simply rest with 'Joe Public' is a crucial and recurring theme of this book.

This must not be taken to suggest that the public at large is inevitably powerless. Helping people to greater control over their lives and health—empowerment—is a cardinal principle of health education, and indeed of health promotion as a whole (see p. 59).

Nor should the definition be construed as representing a 'top-down' or 'medically dominated' model. Two-way communication is envisaged, whereby those traditionally seen as 'providers' and 'recipients' learn from each other, and, as we shall now see, the *'beliefs, attitudes, and behaviour'* referred to above are broader in scope than might at first sight be assumed.

It should be noted that in the ensuing account 'beliefs' are dealt with separately from 'attitudes', for the sake of simplicity. The complex interrelationships between the two are discussed in Chapter 7.

3.1.1 Beliefs

A basic element in the shaping of beliefs is the acquisition of information, and the provision of 'health knowledge' is certainly a fundamental aspect of health education. The breadth of information relevant to health education is well seen in the 'tripartite typology' put forward by Draper *et al.* (1980) as follows.

— *Type 1 health education*: education about the body and how to look after it.
— *Type 2 health education*: provision of information about access to, and the most appropriate use of, health services.
— *Type 3 health education*: education about national, regional, and local policies and structures and processes in the wider environment which are detrimental to health.

As Draper and colleagues have pointed out, the first type is the commonest, and is indispensable for each new generation. Attention to the second has increased in recent times, but has rarely been manifested as an interactive process through which service providers may be educated by service users. The third type tends to be neglected, partly due to the fact that it leads to the path of greatest resistance (by powerful vested interests—see also p. 53), and partly as a result of the 'head-in-the-sand' attitude which denies that health has anything to do with politics.

The strength of a belief may be influenced by such factors as the credibility of an imparter of a 'message' (Section 8.1), the quality and appropriateness of communication (Section 3.5.1), the perceived relevance of a piece of information, and the extent to which a given belief fits in, or clashes, with existing beliefs (see also Section 7.5).

An illustration of human ability to insulate against uncomfortable or inconvenient beliefs is obtained from survey evidence that the majority of cigarette smokers believe that smoking is injurious to health, but that many also express the belief that their continuing to smoke would make no quantitative or qualitative difference to their future experience of illness (OPCS 1983).

So far we have concentrated on beliefs directly concerning health or factors influencing it. The belief system germane to health education includes also beliefs about oneself: self concept is important in shaping perceptions as to one's ability to attain better health. For example, many people become conditioned to see themselves as being 'no good at sports' in such a way as to present a confidence barrier to taking adequate exercise.

3.1.2 Attitudes

Attitudes to health and to health-related factors, such as aspects of lifestyle, are considered in Chapter 7. Health educationists have in recent years been emphasizing the importance of the valuation of self concept—self-esteem—as a determinant of health. People with a high level of self-esteem tend to be aware of their capabilities as individuals, to be relatively socially competent, and to have high resistance to (often unhealthful) pressures to 'conform'. On the other hand, low self-esteem has been linked to difficulties in establishing satisfactory relationships, vulnerability to pressures to conform, and feelings of a lack of control over life.

Thus, it is argued, everyone engaged in educating for health, whether doctors, nurses, school teachers, or others, should do everything possible to promote self-esteem, and must take great care that in-built aspects of their interactions with patients, students, clients, etc. (such as the inherent balance of power) are not allowed to erode it.

3.1.3 Behaviour

This element of the definition of health education naturally includes personal behaviour such as eating, drinking, smoking, and sexual conduct. In saying this, however, it is essential to point out that self-responsibility must be nurtured by helping people to develop health-related lifeskills, such as the ability to make decisions and to be assertive, rather than expecting them simply to take responsibility for their health. Similarly, the behaviour of power-holders, such as politicians and vested business interests, must be fully taken into account. In other words, combining these two points, 'victim-blaming' must be avoided.

The foregoing discussion is built on in later sections of this chapter, and in Part 2 of the book.

3.2 Who are the educators?

It will already have become apparent that many different categories of people have a role to play in health education. The purpose of this section is to discuss the parts played by professionals and agencies specifically charged with health education responsibilities, to examine briefly the role of the mass media, and to relate these to the crucial contributions to be made by workers 'on the ground'.

The establishment in the UK of health education as a profession, and of national health education bodies, can be traced back to the Cohen Report (Ministry of Health 1964).

Health education/promotion officers are now employed by the vast majority of health authorities/boards, and posts are increasingly being established within local authorities and other agencies. Activities on a national scale are the responsibility of the Health Education Authority (for England only—its predecessor, the Health Education Council, having covered also Wales and Northern Ireland), the Health Education Board for Scotland, the Health Promotion Authority for Wales, and the Health Promotion Agency for Northern Ireland.

It is a commonly held belief that national 'campaigns' using mass media are the most important part of health education. This is not so. Experience has shown that such initiatives have a place in putting issues on the public agenda, but that local efforts are vital (Tones 1983; see also p. 117). This is well recognized by the national organizations referred to above, which direct much of their effort to supporting and facilitating grass-roots work.

The principal role of health education/promotion officers (HEOs) is to catalyse health promotion (see Chapter 4) efforts by a whole host of others, and to help them to fulfil their potentials in this direction. HEOs, then, are enablers more than public educators. They help colleagues in other disciplines and other agencies to develop the knowledge, attitudes, and skills required to identify health promotion opportunities in their own sphere of work, and to meet the challenges thus made apparent. The essence of their job is 'training trainers'.

Now that it has been established that the nub of health education is community-based work by a wide range of professionals and others, the theoretical basis of that work will be examined.

3.3 Approaches and ingredients

A large number of classifications and models of health education have been put forward in recent years. The details of these are of most relevance to specialists in the field. In this section and the next, two frameworks for analysis and action are outlined. It is intended that these be taken together with each other and with Chapter 4 in building up a feel for health education and its relationship to health promotion.

The first of these frameworks was developed jointly by a public health physician and a health education officer with experience in working together (Tannahill and Robertson 1986).

Its origins lie in these authors' dissatisfaction with the way in which approaches to health education are commonly distinguished. Discussion often centres on rigidly demarcated 'models' of health education, such as 'medical', 'educational', and 'social' or 'political' models.

Such models tend to be looked upon in either or both of two ways:

(1) as indicative of both a professional and a philosophical under-
     standing of health education, it being expected that a doctor or
     nurse would adhere to the medical model, a teacher to the edu-
     cational model, and so on;

(2) as part of a developmental process, usually represented as a
     sequence from the medical to the educational model (reflecting
     the shift in the professional backgrounds of HEOs from nurs-
     ing to teaching), and often beyond to social or political perspec-
     tives (linked to further changes in HEOs recruitment towards
     social sciences, etc.).

Both of these viewpoints are oversimplified and misleading. Indeed, they are potentially detrimental to the multidisciplinary practice of health education, through perpetuating counter-productive stereotypes and detracting from professional development and collaboration.

Health education theory and practice have always had medical, educational, and other components, and it is better to look at the evolutionary sequence in terms of changes in all of the various ingredients of the health education 'cake' and in the overall 'mix' than to sustain false distinctions between inevitably interlinking classical models.

Accordingly, approaches to health education may be classified as *traditional*, *transitional*, and *modern*.

3.3.1 Traditional approach (Fig. 3.1)

The traditional approach to health education has a negative focus, that is to say it is aimed fairly and squarely at prevention rather than addressing positive health.

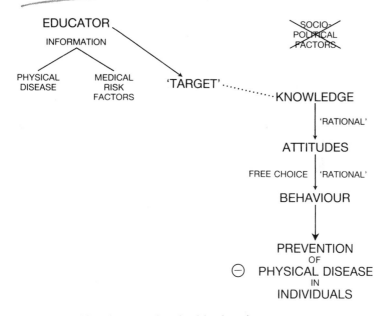

Fig 3.1   Traditional approach to health education.

The main emphasis is on *physical* aspects of ill-health. This is reflected in the information base used, which represents a highly limited medical perspective.

Similarly, the educational basis is narrow. *Information* is provided by *educators* in the expectation of an *orderly sequence* from knowledge through attitudes to (medically defined) 'correct' behaviour. The notion of 'rational man' is implied.

Social and political determinants of health are neglected. People are considered to be *free to choose* their health-related behaviour.

Efforts are directed at *targeted individuals*. The collective dimension of health is not addressed.

3.3.2 Transitional approach

Recognition that the idea of a straightforward knowledge—attitudes—behaviour sequence was misguided led to a dependence on manipulative, 'irrational' tactics, intended to shock or scare people into behaving 'sensibly'. Thus such unlikely images as skulls smoking cigarettes were presented to the public, to very limited effect.

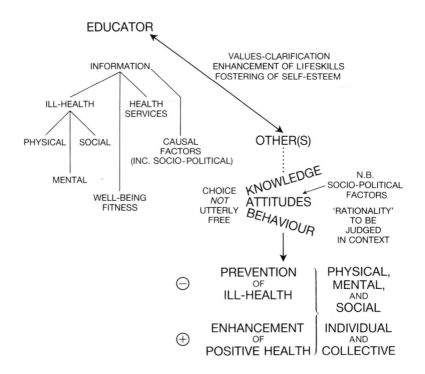

Fig 3.2 Modern approach to health education.

3.3.3 Modern approach (Fig. 3.2)

This approach is more cumbersome to represent diagrammatically as it takes into account the complexity of health and the factors which influence it, and of modern educational theory and practice.

It can seen from Fig. 3.2 that the modern approach to health education is explicitly aimed not only at prevention but also at the promotion of *positive health*.

Furthermore, both positive and negative dimensions of health are seen as having *physical, mental and social* facets (in accordance with Chapter 2). This leads to a widening out of the 'content' of health education in line with the Draper *et al.* (1980) typology (see Section 3.1.1).

The educational framework is likewise broader, in acceptance of the abundant evidence that mere provision of information is not enough, that there is no tidy and inevitable step-wise progression from knowledge through attitudes to behaviour. The educational process here involves helping people to clarify their values (in relation to themselves, health, health-influencing behaviour, etc.; see also Chapter 9) and to acquire various *lifeskills* (see p. 30), with an emphasis on fostering their *self-esteem*.

Linked to this, the education process is *participatory*. Communication is *two-way*. The 'educator' ensures that the other(s) are able to express their knowledge and opinions, and respects and values these. In this way an understanding of people's perspectives, based on their life experiences, may be obtained, this being infinitely preferable to assaulting people with unsympathetic views of 'correctness' dependent on a medical judgement of 'rationality' (see also Chapter 8.).

Major *constraints to freedom of choice* in health-related behaviour are acknowledged. The effects of socio-political factors on health are recognized, and efforts are made to secure a climate more conducive to good health (see also pp. 42, 59).

Collective dimensions to health, behaviour, and health education are seen as important.

Although a developmental sequence has been presented, it has to be admitted that practice has not uniformly kept pace with principles. In schools, for instance, a great deal of sound curriculum development work has yet to reach many classrooms. Even HEOs have often found it difficult to move on from the traditional mode: in part this reflects the difficulties faced by chronically

understaffed, underfunded, and undervalued health education/
promotion units in trying to operate proactively rather than being
forced to react to the often inappropriate and conflicting expectations of other, often more powerful, professional groups.

Wider awareness of the modern approach amongst the many occupational groups with a part to play would accelerate progress in
health education, both through the direct benefits of various disciplines' pulling together and through the resultant shift to an
environment which facilitates the activities and proper development
of specialist health education/promotion services.

Key aspects of the approach advocated will become clearer on
reading the next section, following which the implications for practice will be explored. Before moving on to the next theoretical
framework, however, it is helpful to look in more detail at the
question of freedom of choice, using cigarette smoking as an
illustration.

Doctors, nurses, and others often speak and act as though
smokers are stupid people who have freely opted for a course of
action which stands a high chance of making them ill and shortening
their lives. (Indeed this attitude has, in recent times, been
extended as far as questioning smokers' rights for free treatment
under the National Health Service.) Committed smokers themselves, perhaps out of denial that they can be controlled by 'the
dreaded weed', frequently collaborate in the perpetuation of such
victim-blaming by insisting that they have freely and willingly
chosen to smoke.

Imagine a society in which there is no mythological imagery
surrounding cigarette smoking: no spurious association with man-
liness, elegance, sophistication, achievement, 'grown-upness',
smartness, and so on; where there is open portrayal in tobacco
advertising (if it exists at all) that cigarettes are dirty and smelly, and
that smoking kills around one in seven of the population; where
there are decent health education programmes from cradle to grave;
where it is acknowledged that tobacco does not soothe the nerves
until one is already 'hooked' on it; where no other false values are
attached to smoking; and where there are no social pressures to
smoke. Suppose that in this environment an adult wakes up one day
and announces that, having weighed up all the pros and cons, he or
she has arrived at the unfettered decision to take up smoking 20
cigarettes daily for life, thereby running a one in four risk of dying
prematurely. One might reasonably say that that person has freely

chosen to smoke (or else that he or she must be mad!).

Real life is, of course, very different. False images and distorted values in relation to smoking are nurtured by misleading, sophisticated advertising campaigns, through sponsorship (including that of sports events and even of medical research!), by other means of media portrayal (for instance in 'soap operas'), by peer pressure ('if you don't smoke you're a wally', etc.), by role models, and so on. Moreover, decisions to start smoking are generally taken by minors (whom society considers to have little competence to make other important decisions). Also, of course, the practice is habit-forming: as McKeown (1976) pointed out so elegantly: 'Our habits commonly begin as pleasures of which we have no need and end as necessities in which we have no pleasure.' Add to all this the relationship between smoking and socio-economic disadvantage, and we have powerful arguments that the concept of freedom of choice in this context is seriously flawed, somewhat offensive, and rather dangerous. Some or all of these arguments apply to many other aspects of health-related behaviour, as diverse as taking other drugs (such as alcohol and illicit substances), eating, and even driving (witness the growth of a 'speed' culture, fuelled by the aggressive marketing of high-performance cars, and advertisements such as the one which invites us to 'test fly one tomorrow').

3.4 Orientations

The framework just presented serves to broaden our views on how an individual, or a particular profession, might go about educating for health (and being educated for health). Another way of examining the evolution of health education will now be proposed. It is principally concerned with how the planning and organization of health education programmes should be undertaken, but also serves to reinforce previously presented theory in a practical way. This framework is categorized according to various possible orientations for health education.

3.4.1 Disease-orientated (Fig. 3.3)

This type of health education is still very common, largely due to the combined forces of epidemiologists, politicians, and health service managers.

Efforts are aimed at the prevention of specific diseases, and there is much emphasis on gauging success in terms of progress towards target rates of morbidity and mortality. The inherent assumption is that major preventable diseases, such as cardiovascular disorders and malignancies, are best dealt with by specific preventive programmes aimed at reducing relevant 'risk factors' (factors which confer an increased likelihood of developing particular diseases).

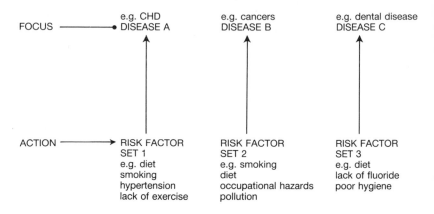

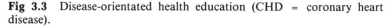

Fig 3.3   Disease-orientated health education (CHD = coronary heart disease).

The focus is thus negative. People are expected to 'look after themselves' in the light of anti-cancer 'campaigns' and the like. In fact, this kind of approach is of limited educational validity. Whilst it is true that people who are already primed to make changes, such as stopping smoking or cutting down on alcohol, may well do so as a result of anti-tobacco or anti-alcohol publicity or advice, it is arguably unrealistic to expect wholesale changes in lifestyle as a result of purely negatively focused education. Why should people give up valued practices (for example smoking, drinking to excess, eating too many chips, or simply being slothful), or embark on new ones which are perceived as nasty or even painful (such as eating a healthful diet or taking exercise), on the strength of some speculative, intangible future benefit?

This consideration becomes especially pressing when one considers those in society who have the greatest health needs, for whom the present is a bitter struggle, pleasures are few (and often damaging), and there is little perception of a future worth investing in, or indeed even open to personal influence.

Further problems arise from the incrementalist nature of this approach to formulating health education programmes. What tends to happen is that individuals or groups work on single topics in relative, or even absolute, isolation from one another. Turning to the examples in Fig. 3.3, then, we may find that there is in a single community a coronary heart disease (CHD) prevention programme, one aimed at preventing cancers, and another concerned with dental disease. Those involved in each separate initiative are faced with the prospect of making an impact across the community. As a result, key 'gate-keepers' to the community may be swamped by individual demands: the head-teacher in a given school, for example, may feel besieged by separate requests for inclusion in an already crowded timetable. Furthermore, given the overlap in risk factors for many types of disease (see Fig 3.3), there will inevitably be considerable duplication of effort, which, as well as being wasteful, may lead to over-saturation and a community 'switch-off' response. Worse still, there is a considerable propensity for inconsistency of 'messages'. For instance 'CHD preventers' may throw up their hands in horror at dental colleagues who may encourage children to eat fatty, salty crisps (rather than sugary snacks). Such professional inconsistency leads to public confusion and militates against behavioural change.

Another source of potentially damaging inconsistency lies in the scope there is for pragmatism to be eclipsed by epidemiological purity: trivial scientific nit-picking and professional point-scoring may distract from large areas of consensus (CHD prevention being a case in point).

Criticism can also be levelled at the fact that this is an 'expert-dominated' orientation. To draw an analogy with clinical practice, health professionals provide population 'diagnoses' and mass 'prescriptions'—without any community 'consultations'. Ordinary people are expected to 'comply' even though they may not agree with the diagnoses or see the prescriptions as being appropriate.

Finally, the disease-orientated model is fundamentally deficient in its incomplete view of health, not only in neglecting social and collective aspects but also in ignoring the position dimension.

3.4.2 Risk factor-orientated (Fig. 3.4)

This is aimed at eliminating particular risk factors in order to prevent associated diseases. Much health education is currently focused in this way.

The main advantage of this approach over the disease orientation is in the recognition that a single risk factor can be linked to more than one disease category. With reference to examples shown in Fig. 3.4, a smoking prevention programme can stress associations with lung and other cancers, as well as CHD (and, of course, chronic bronchitis, emphysema, etc.); efforts can be directed at encouraging a low-risk diet, taking into account the many and varied links between food and ill-health. Thus, although the model is still an incrementalist one, there are fewer problems with duplication and confusion.

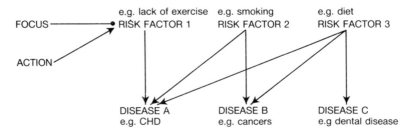

Fig 3.4   Risk factor-orientated health education (CHD = coronary heart disease).

However, the model is open to the other criticisms levelled at disease-orientated health education: the view of health is inadequate; educational soundness is limited; and experts dominate. Indeed the two orientations taken together are clearly reminiscent of the 'traditional approach' to health education described earlier (see p. 33).

3.4.3 Health-orientated (Fig. 3.5)

Here there is a dual focus: the aim is to enhance positive health as well as to prevent ill-health. The physical, mental, and social components of both of these dimensions of health are recognized.

The incorporation of a positive focus makes for greater educational validity. People are more likely to adopt a particular lifestyle if it appears attractive. For instance, a healthful diet is presented as rich, varied, and enjoyable, rather than as something Calvinistic and inevitably less palatable than 'chips with everything'. Similarly, exercise is promoted largely on the grounds that it makes people feel

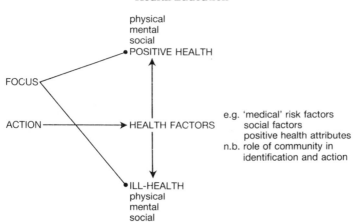

Fig 3.5   Health-orientated health education.

good, instead of being painted as a painful chore. Preventive benefits are not ignored, but these are regarded as additional to effects
on well-being and fitness.

Such an outlook is only common sense when we think of our own
motivations in life. We like to do things which are appealing and
enjoyable, and which give us tangible and relatively fast benefits; if
at the same time we are increasing our chances of avoiding illness or
dying before our time, then so much the better. A moment's thought
as to how potentially damaging products and practices are promoted further reinforces the argument (think, for example, of
advertisements linking alcohol with glamour, sophistication, and
success, with no hint of the possibility of making a fool or nuisance
of oneself socially, or of the impairment of performance which
comes with inappropriate use; see also p. 37).

It should be noted that Fig. 3.5 refers to 'ill-health' rather than
diseases. This acknowledges the need to go beyond the technical
notion of disease (see Chapter 2). The distinction can be illustrated
by referring to the fact that a relatively high proportion of medical
consultations are, in doctors' eyes, trivial or even unnecessary,
whereas presenting patients may feel otherwise. Another example is
that someone may experience a level of mental ill-health which is
highly significant to his or her life, even if it falls short of qualifying
for a medical label as a psychiatric illness.

The 'health factors' referred to naturally do include 'medical' risk
factors, but they go beyond these. Instead of dealing with individual

aspects of lifestyle *in vacuo*, the model properly acknowledges underlying circumstances, including social factors. Common links in the origins of many types of health-damaging behaviour are recognized—for example peer and other social pressures (such as those arising out of multiple deprivation)—in relation to the use of alcohol, tobacco, and other drugs. In other words, a holistic view of health and its determinants prevails, and programmes are less incrementalist, and more likely to be well co-ordinated, than is the case with the disease and risk-factor orientations.

The health factors include also attributes discussed earlier in the account of the 'modern approach' to health education (see p. 35), and in the clarification of the 'behaviour' element of the definition of health education (see p. 30), qualities which contribute directly to true well-being as well as protecting against ill-health. These positive health attributes are just as applicable on the scale of a whole community as at the level of the individual. Thus a community can be helped to acquire a higher level of self-esteem and a set of empowering skills, skills which help it to take greater control both over its health as a collective entity and over that of its individual members.

The above principles are central to the so-called community development approach to health education. So also is another feature of the health-orientated model, namely community sensitivity and participation. Rather than operating purely on a professionally set agenda, the public, whether individually (for example in doctor—patient consultations) or collectively (for instance as part of a community of individuals) are involved in identifying health factors and priorities, and in shaping and securing action. Sensitivity and participation are likewise very important when working with individuals and small groups.

3.5 Implications of theory for practice

Although there are clear areas of overlap between the two theoretical frameworks put forward in this chapter, their practical implications differ to an extent, as has already been indicated. The health education 'approaches' framework has an important bearing on the way in which individual health educators and professional groups (doctors, nurses, environmental health officers, teachers, etc.) operate—and in particular communicate. The set of health education 'orientations', whilst impinging in a similar way on individual practice, is of greatest significance in relation to the way in which programmes of health education are designed and delivered in the community.

This being so, the practical implications of the theory presented will be considered further under two headings: communication and programme planning.

3.5.1 Communication

The importance of two-way communication in health education was stressed in the account of the 'modern' approach to health education. Only through a participatory process may health professionals and other potential health educators find out what makes their 'clients' tick. Only thus may the educators avoid falling into the trap of imposing on the clients an inappropriate, professionally defined model of 'rationality'.

Consider the situation of a woman, pregnant for the seventh time. The family struggles to exist on State benefits, in the absence of paid employment. To the doctor confirming this latest pregnancy, the addition of yet another mouth to feed and body to clothe might well appear irrational. To the mother-to-be, the pregnancy may be highly valued: her six existing children might all be girls or boys, and she may yearn for a child of the other sex; alternatively, motherhood might be the only aspect of her life which has made her feel important and fulfilled. Who is the more 'rational'—the woman or her doctor?

The above illustration is, of course, something of a caricature of what in reality can be much more subtle contrasts between professional and lay perspectives. These differences can only be teased out through a 'partnership' (rather than 'provider-recipient') model of communication. In adopting this style of interaction, any 'messages' subsequently 'delivered' by the professional are more likely to be—and be perceived as—relevant to the 'client', and are thus more likely to be acted upon. The attendant treating of adults as adults, and of people's views as important rather than insignificant, helps to encourage 'adult' behaviour and fosters self-esteem.

To what extent does this model prevail in practice? An important study towards answering this was carried out in a general medical practice setting, but is undoubtedly relevant to a wide range of professionals. The 'Patient Project', carried out by the Health

Education Studies Unit (1982) for the then Health Education Council, involved an intensive study of a large number of GP consultations. The aim was to explore how health education could facilitate public participation in informed debate about health issues. A number of the findings were favourable and highlighted the scope for informed decision-making and the sharing of lay and medical viewpoints. However, there was little to suggest that this potential was being tapped. Problems were found to arise from doctors' failing to explore patients' thinking frameworks, and a particularly notable finding was a tendency for the atmosphere in consultations to take a turn for the worse when patients sought to participate rather than being passive junior partners.

These findings are perhaps understandable, given the pedagogic way in which medical students and doctors are taught, and taught to teach. This does not, however, make the problems any less critical. One has to take very seriously the conclusions of the researchers that opportunistic health education by GPs might be dangerous as things stand, and that efforts should be concentrated on helping practitioners to develop core communication skills, rather on specific aspects of health education and prevention.

It has to be acknowledged that medical schools and GP vocational training schemes have recognized the need for communication training. However, it is fair to say that in general there has, to date, been too little attention to the incorporation of lay feedback into such training.

Attempts to develop communication skills must give due recognition to the subtlety and complexity of the communication process. An understanding of some of the most significant pitfalls may be gained by breaking the process up into a number of stages.

Let us consider one side of a two-way interaction—communication from a doctor to a patient. This component of the communication process may be simplified as a sequence as follows.

Delivery ⟶ *receipt* ⟶ *comprehension* ⟶ *interpretation*

The extent to which information delivered is received is influenced by the quantity and concentration of information given, and by the language used. The doctor's language may be alien to the patient, not just because of professional jargon but also on account of social class and general educational differences. At a simpler level, of course, receipt is affected also by volume and clarity of enunciation, coupled with acuteness of hearing.

Comprehension following successful delivery and receipt of words is also critically affected by language. It is helpful for the doctor to check comprehension. However, even if this is done, and both doctor and patient are happy that a message has been given and successfully received, the interpretation of that message by the patient (and hence subsequent action) may well be seriously different from that intended by the doctor. Interpretation is influenced by linguistic factors and by thinking frameworks.

The distinction between comprehension and interpretation may be demonstrated through an exaggerated scenario, as follows. Suppose a doctor gives a woman a packet of oral contraceptives, telling her that if she takes them she will not become pregnant. The woman might 'understand' the instructions but interpret them as meaning that the packet is in some way a talisman controlling fertility, such that the act of taking the pills from the doctor (rather than ingesting them) is the crucial contraceptive step.

In checking understanding, then, asking the question 'Do you understand?' is not enough: interpretation must be properly ascertained, and patients' thinking frameworks (which may differ substantially from those of professionals) explored.

Superimposed on the above sequence, and having a bearing on the consequences of an episode of communication, is the question of retention of information. The quality of recall by patients has been found to be a barrier to subsequent action by some researchers (Ley *et al.* 1976), but did not seem to be a major problem in the Patient Project. Nevertheless, professionals must endeavour to ensure that their communication style makes for good retention.

In moving beyond the communication sequence, two further steps may be defined—intention and action. Behavioural intention following an interaction is determined, in part, by the elements considered above—language, understanding, retention, etc. Perceived relevance is also significant: 'messages' must be couched in an appropriate way, based on a knowledge of the patient's background and thinking framework. Justification by the professional of recommended action, in line with this thinking framework, is important in motivational terms.

Even then there may well be barriers to desired action, perhaps economic, social, or related to dependence. The professional must acquaint him/herself with these barriers, so that the patient can see that his/her position is well understood, and in order to work with the 'client' towards overcoming the obstacles.

So far we have concentrated on the verbal aspects of communication. It is, however, well known that non-verbal communication is vitally important. Returning once more to the GP situation, keeping a patient waiting, avoiding eye-contact, prematurely writing a prescription, appearing distracted or uninterested, having a patronizing demeanour, or presenting a cluttered desk as a barricade may well detract utterly from even the most skilful use of words.

Doctors and other professionals have an advantage in the non-verbal area as regards the credibility and importance emanating from professional power. Another, more personal, type of power which may impinge on an interaction is charismatic power. Even the perceived attractiveness of a communicator may have significant effects. Finally, communication is more likely to be successful if the 'client' sees that the professional has some important characteristics in common with him/herself, although genuine empathy can make up for a lack of this (see also Section 8.1.).

Before leaving this section, it is important to remind the reader that the above represents an analysis of one side of the process of communication. The factors and elements described and discussed operate also in the other direction, from 'client' to professional. The purpose of spelling this out is not to overwhelm the reader with the convolutions of communication (the problems *can* be overcome) but rather to stress once more the importance of a participatory, two-way, model of communication.

Although the emphasis in this account has been on one-to-one communication, the same basic principles hold for individuals or teams of professionals working with groups or whole communities.

3.5.2 Programme planning

The logical conclusion from our advocacy of 'health-orientated' health education (pp. 40–2) is that health education programmes should be planned primarily according to opportunities for engaging in a dialogue with individuals and collections of people in the community, through prioritizing by key setting and key group instead of disease or risk factor topic (Tannahill 1990). As well as being philosophically preferable, this is desirable from an organizational point of view: it gives rise to co-ordinated programmes in a given situation, rather than a 'hotch-potch' of topics (such as cancers, alcohol, etc.) slotted in in an incrementalist manner (see p. 39).

The key settings and key groups are best selected locally, for maximum sensitivity to a given community's needs. Examples of key settings are primary health care, hospitals, schools, other educational institutions, the workplace, and deprived communities (notably through the community development approach: see p. 42). Key groups include old people, unemployed people, parents, and ethnic minority groups. Programmes of health education should be tailored to the special needs of the particular settings and groups, to ensure relevant and appropriate inputs in relation to age, circumstances, and people's own priorities. Such programmes should also make full use of the vast network of potential health educators in the community.

In a number of situations, single-topic education initiatives (those concerned with one particular aspect of ill-health or risk) *are* appropriate. Examples include: agenda setting (raising the level of awareness of the significance of a health problem, such as CHD, or of a risk factor, for instance, smoking); responding to new or urgent threats to health (for example the acquired immune deficiency syndrome—AIDS); promotion of the uptake of specific preventive services (immunization, screening, etc.); opportunistic education (for instance, advice to individual smokers to give up); education aimed at preventing the progression or recurrence of illness; advocacy of specific policies aimed at protecting health (see p. 58); and reacting to certain needs identified by the community.

It is, however, important to ensure that single-topic efforts are complementary to, and set within the context of, comprehensive programmes of education in the identified key settings and groups. For example, AIDS-specific work must take into account existing health education programmes, and efforts must be made to incorporate such topic-specific work into broad-based health education programmes while the acute educational emergency is being dealt with. Also, advantage should be taken of opportunities to broaden out from topic-specific initiatives in given settings or groups.

Finally, comprehensive programmes throughout the community will, of course, entail specific inputs on lifestyle, disease, etc. The crucial feature is that such programmes are developed systematically, in a co-ordinated manner, with recognition of the shared roots of various aspects of health-related behaviour, and with sensitivity to local public perceptions and perspectives, instead of growing haphazardly from a purely professionally defined base.

3.6 Conclusions

1. Health education seeks to enhance positive health and to prevent or diminish ill-health, through influencing beliefs, attitudes, and behaviour. The stimulation of a healthful environment—social and political as well as physical—is an important objective.

2. Health education must reach power-holders in society rather than just the general public. Moreover, it must contribute to the empowerment of ordinary members of the community, through developing lifeskills and fostering self-esteem.

3. Many professionals and agencies have a part to play in health education/promotion. Health education/promotion officers can help them to develop their roles.

4. Mass media initiatives are of value, but the nub of health education is community-based work.

5. Traditional, transitional, and modern approaches to health education may be distinguished. Practice has not uniformly kept pace with advances in theory.

6. The modern approach uses a broad information base and sound educational principles, and recognizes the importance of socio-political factors in health and health-related behaviour. It is a participatory model.

7. An evolutionary process in health education—from disease-orientated, through risk factor-orientated, to health-orientated —may be described. Once again we find that practice has lagged behind principles.

8. The health-orientated approach is preferable on both philosophical and organizational grounds. It requires the development of comprehensive, community-sensitive, and participatory programmes of health education in key settings and with key groups in the community, rather than programmes centred around disease or hazard topics.

9. Comprehensive community programmes of health education should be complemented by more specific initiatives, as appropriate.

4 Health promotion

Having explored the field of health education in some detail in Chapter 3, we shall now consider two more expressions—'prevention' and 'health protection'—before moving on to define 'health promotion'.

4.1 Prevention

Central to prevention is the notion of reducing the risk of occurrence of a disease process, illness, injury, disability, handicap, or some other unwanted phenomenon or state. More detailed definition of the term is customarily left to its classification as 'primary', 'secondary' and 'tertiary', the value of which lies in its reminding us of the scope for prevention after the first onset of a particular health problem. Unfortunately there are a number of drawbacks associated with this nomenclature.

First, a review of the literature (Tannahill 1985a) indicates that there is no standard definition of the three levels of prevention: particulars differ significantly. A shorthand vocabulary in such a situation is thus unhelpful and hazardous: the labels 'primary', 'secondary' and 'tertiary' used alone, in the absence of unanimity of meaning, become worthless.

Second, the classification focuses on *disease*, the most glaring exclusion being the area of family planning, which most people would consider to be an important aspect of prevention (of social and mental ill-health, for instance).

Third, the various schemes used include, whether by implication or explicit statement, *treatment* of ill-health. For example, 'secondary prevention' has been defined as 'the treatment and cure of established disease' (Alderson 1976). Thus just about everything a doctor does could be construed as prevention. It is self-evident that treatment is aimed at the prevention of certain consequences of ill-health (such as death), but the blurring of distinctions between prevention and cure and palliation in this way is undesirable: it renders meaningless present-day political and professional rhetoric in favour of prevention.

The benefits of the traditional approach to classification can be preserved, and the problems lessened, by discarding convenient tags which allow us to speak without making our meanings clear (even to ourselves), and describing instead four foci for prevention, as follows.

1. *Prevention of the onset or first manifestation of a disease process, or some other first occurrence, through risk reduction.* Taking coronary heart disease as an illustration, this includes efforts to avoid high blood cholesterol levels, to discourage smoking, and to maintain or secure an adequately low blood pressure. Accident prevention through reducing hazards or risk-taking behaviour is another example. Broadened out from matters of disease, this category includes, for example, the avoidance of a first unwanted pregnancy through contraception.

2. *Prevention of the progression of a disease process or other unwanted state, through early detection when this favourably affects outcome.* In relation to disease, this includes methods of picking up precursor or presymptomatic stages of particular conditions (such as screening for premalignant changes in the cervix and for early breast cancer, respectively). Although the treatment of discovered abnormalities is clearly an essential component, it is early detection that is the true preventive step. Returning to the case of unwanted pregnancy, detection of an unwelcome fetus (whether abnormal or normal) at a stage which permits termination of pregnancy fits here.

3. *Prevention of avoidable complications of an irreversible, manifest disease or some other unwanted state.* In the interests of meaningful and commonsense distinction between prevention and treatment, this excludes, for example, the medical or surgical management of angina or the control of blood glucose levels in diabetes. Measures aimed at minimizing indirect consequences of an illness are, on the other hand, included—an example being attempts to prevent pressure sores or urinary tract infections in multiple sclerosis. Arrangements for the adoption of an unwanted child might be included here.

4. *Prevention of the recurrence of an illness or other unwanted phenomenon.* Examples include efforts to prevent a second heart attack or unwanted pregnancy.

It has to be admitted that this system of classification is less than ideal. Perfection is impossible to achieve when seeking to reduce the continua of diseases' natural histories to a set of man-made compartments, and distinctions between prevention and treatment, however desirable, are inevitably arbitrary and superficial. Nevertheless, it is hoped that the essence of the philosophy and practice of prevention can be gleaned from it and that at least the reader has been made aware of the undesirability of loose use of vocabulary against such a complex background.

Given the existence of a number of excellent publications dealing with the subject, it is not intended to go into the principles of preventive medicine any further in this book, except insofar as to set it in the context of health promotion (see p. 58).

4.2 Health protection

This can be seen as the descendant of the great old regulatory public health measures which have had such an impact on the population's health over the last century. It may be defined as follows.

Health protection comprises legal or fiscal controls, other regulations and policies, and voluntary codes of practice, aimed at the enhancement of positive health and the prevention of ill-health.

Health protection makes it less likely that people will encounter hazards in the environment, and that they will behave in an unhealthful manner, while increasing their chances of living in a positively healthful environment and having a lifestyle which promotes positive health. (It is the wider environment—political, legislative, social, etc., as well as physical—which is referred to here.) In other words, it is about making healthy choices easier choices.

The concept, and barriers to regulatory action, will now be illustrated through a series of examples, following which ethical considerations will be briefly explored.

4.2.1 Legal control

Examples include legislation concerning: the wearing of seat-belts in cars; the sale of alcohol and tobacco to minors; drinking and driving; the control of communicable diseases; and health and safety at work.

4.2.2 Fiscal control

A recent example of pro-health fiscal policy in the UK has been the imposition of differential taxation on petrol to make the unleaded variety cheaper, as an inducement to motorists to convert to this type of fuel in the interest of environmental protection.

No Government has, however, had consistent and strong fiscal policies for health protection. Duties on tobacco and alcohol have been of particular concern to the pro-health lobby. It is widely accepted that the health problems associated with tobacco and alcohol in a society correlate with the levels of use of these drugs in that society, and that, over time, usage is inversely related to real price (ASH *et al.* 1988; FCM 1988). (The link between alcohol price and consumption has been demonstrated even for problem drinkers; Kendell *et al.* 1983.) This is the rationale for widespread calls to increase alcohol and tobacco taxation (which forms a high proportion of the retail prices of these commodities) on health grounds. These calls have met with limited success. Despite occasional health-motivated increases in duty, smoking and drinking remain cheaper practices (in real terms) than 40 years ago, when knowledge of ill-effects was less advanced.

4.2.3 Other regulations and policies

Regulatory action is not the exclusive province of Government. In recent years, for example, many employers (including health authorities/boards, who have a special exemplar role) have developed policies to promote non-smoking on their premises. Workplace policies on alcohol and problem drinking have also been becoming more common, as have canteen food policies.

So far we have concentrated on specific hazards, such as tobacco and alcohol. We should, however, remember that more fundamental aspects of public policy-making, such as those relating to housing, education, employment, and the prevention and alleviation of poverty, impinge on health. Health protection policies can address the full range of 'prerequisites for health' as identified by WHO (p. 62).

4.2.4 Voluntary codes

These are in general poor substitutes for compulsion. The promotion and advertising of cigarettes, for instance, is regulated by a process of agreement between the tobacco industry and the Government, and breaches of the resulting voluntary code have been so frequent, and in many instances so crass, as to become legendary (Roberts 1986; 1987).

4.2.5 Barriers to health protection

A major barrier to national regulatory action in favour of health appears to be a simple process of neglect—failure to look for, and give priority to, likely health consequences of public policy, such as fiscal policy. The 'Skoal Bandits' affair (p. 83) is perhaps a demonstration of what can happen when there is no proper mechanism for gearing action by the various Departments of the Government towards the protection of the nation's health.

Another problem is perceived clashes of the interest between Government Departments. Thus, it is often argued, deterrent increases in tobacco taxation are not overall in the national interest since tobacco revenue is the country's third largest source of income (after Value Added Tax and oil). In short, we cannot afford successfully to discourage smoking with any rapidity, especially as many more people might then live to collect their pensions.

This line of argument may be countered in three ways. Firstly, an economic analysis of a package of anti-smoking measures (including a rise in duty), based on a predicted 40 per cent resultant reduction in smoking, has suggested that, as well as saving many lives and much misery, the measures would result in an increase in Government revenue income from the higher prices paid by the remaining smokers (Atkinson and Townsend 1977). Secondly, and more fundamentally, taxation is transferable: the same amount of revenue may be obtained by taxing something else (such as income), and so the case for the economic imperative of smoking is spurious. Thirdly, it is surely unacceptable for public policy (even if the economic reasoning were sounder) to preserve the status quo whereby one in seven deaths in England and Wales, for example, results from smoking. A national policy of compulsory euthanasia at retirement age would be a more honest, equitable, and effective means of achieving the desired economic objective!

The third barrier to health protection nationally stems from the enormous power of vested interests over public policy-making. Big business is in a strong position to oppose pro-health policies and perpetuate unhealthful ones, in the interests of profit. It is widely stated that progress towards a sensible, coherent food policy, for instance, is persistently hampered by the influence of the food and agricultural industries.

The impact of Industry on policies which affect health is very clearly seen in relation to tobacco. The Zoos Bill episode of 1981 (Anonymous 1981) is a case in point. More than 100 amendments to this hitherto uncontroversial Private Member's Bill suddenly materialized, with the result that another Bill, aimed at giving the Government power to control tobacco promotion, ran out of Parliamentary time. The latter had been expected to gain a majority. The amendments to the Zoos Bill were tabled by a handful of Members of Parliament (MPs), one of the principal participants being a parliamentary adviser to a major tobacco company, and others also having direct or indirect links with the industry. Not surprisingly this incident has been seen as a case of filibustering (an obstruction of legislation through delaying tactics) in which health lost out to darker motives. This raises the question of links between MPs and vested interests which damage health. These may be directly financial (through appointments with tobacco, alcohol, or related public-relations companies) or may involve constituency or trade union interests in industries. Contributions to political party funds might also be seen as potentially significant.

Political influence at the national level is reinforced by the power of vested interests over the public and the media. Power over the public is exerted by control over the availability and pricing of products for consumers (health education cannot succeed if advocated healthful goods cannot be found or afforded), by marketing strategies, and so on. Power over the media may take the form of lucrative advertising accounts 'with strings attached' (such as hints to magazines that business will be taken elsewhere if, say, anti-smoking features appear), of misinformation, and so forth.

These illustrations of constraints to health protection nationally are matched by interferences at more local levels. The raising of awareness of such local and national obstacles is an important component of type 3 health education as described by Draper et al. (p. 29). Given the enormity and power of the opposition it is easy to see why this type of work tends to be neglected.

It is, however, heartening to see professional bodies, such as the British Medical Association and the Royal College of Physicians of London, campaigning for health protection measures (BMA 1986).

4.2.6 Ethical considerations

In many instances, attempts are made to justify antipathy to health protection on ethical grounds. Thus, it is often argued, it would be wrong to exert compulsory control on tobacco advertising or sponsorship because people's freedom of choice would be restricted. The issue of free rational choice in health-related behaviour has already been considered in some detail (see p. 37), and on the basis of that discussion it is suggested here that the concept should be treated with scepticism. Failure to regulate powerful concerns which damage health serves to perpetuate the freedom of choice of those with a great deal of power (major business and others with vested interests in unhealthful products or activities) to exploit those with relatively little (the public).

In any case, society accepts a great deal of regulation for the common good: it is illogical that the manufacturers of cigarettes, the major preventable cause of serious illness and premature death, and alcohol, with its immense direct and indirect impact on social, mental, and physical health, should be treated so lightly (see Chapter 10). The contrast with the treatment of illicit drugs is striking; no-one, of course, makes a public case for the protection of heroin barons, for instance.

One specific ethical dilemma worth looking at here is the question of taxation of tobacco and alcohol products. The pro-health lobby often demands sharp and steep rises, outstripping inflation. In doing so they often meet the highly valid counter-argument that swingeing increases would hit the poorest most. It would be highly desirable if the question of large increases in duty were to be debated publicly. In the meantime, however, it would seem reasonable to take regular fiscal action such that the products do not become any cheaper in real terms.

4.3 A model of health promotion

We are now, at last, in a position to reflect on the meaning of 'health promotion'. Although the term has been in existence for many years, it came to the fore during the 1980s, and it is currently highly fashionable in professional and political circles.

Given this popularity, it is most unfortunate that 'health promotion' is used in a number of different ways, even by the same people. The problem is accentuated by the fact that the term tends to be bandied about somewhat glibly, without clarification of underlying meanings. As with health education, therefore, it is perfectly possible—and indeed by no means uncommon—for two people, or even an entire committee or conference, to have a discussion about health promotion and be referring to very different things.

It is helpful at this stage to look at a number of interpretations which have been put forward in recent years, noting how these vary in scope and detail.

Health promotion has frequently been taken to cover attempts to promote positive health. This interpretation has often been implied rather than explicit: there has, for instance, been a tendency to talk or write of 'health promotion and disease prevention' as a sort of inseparable coupling, without making clear the perceived differences between the two expressions.

Some have made an explicit distinction between health promotion and prevention (NALGO 1984; WHO 1984; Nutbeam 1986). The value of this, however well-argued the case, is markedly diminished by the fact that most people would see health education as central to health promotion, and at the same time health education tends to be treated largely (or even exclusively) as a subset of prevention. Moreover, research into what has been written and done by health promotion groups, professional bodies, etc. under that banner of health promotion reveals that preventive activities, such as immunization and screening, are highly prominent.

Reference was made above to the commonly perceived place of health education in relation to health promotion. In fact many people seem to equate the two terms. This confusing trend has been aggravated by moves by numerous individual health education officers and units (endorsed by the now Society of Health Education and Promotion Specialists) towards changing their professional label to health promotion, generally without any clearly stated redefinition of role. This has had the unfortunate side-effect of blurring the specific *educational* expertise and contribution of this professional group as the ill-defined, but nonetheless dazzling, band-wagon of health promotion has gained momentum with all and sundry clamouring to climb aboard.

Even more unsatisfactory is the interpretation of health promotion as that part of health education which involves high-profile mass media inputs, with connotations of 'razzmatazz'. This arises from what we see as a misunderstanding of the 'promotion' component of the term as having to do with marketing or selling (as opposed to enhancing or nurturing) health, and has at times gone as far as health service managers and others referring to 'health promotions' and 'health promotions officers'. The problem with this popular misapprehension is that, at a time when health promotion is stressed as important, left, right, and centre, the importance of this type of activity is grossly overplayed at the expense of sound educational principles (p. 31).

There are other, broader views of health promotion. Thus the term has often been used as an 'umbrella' covering health education and 'social engineering' (through fiscal, legal, and other environmental manipulations) (Tones 1983). Where the term is used in this wider manner, health promotion is frequently defined as a list of ingredients, without examination of their interconnections.

It has even been commonplace to use such a broad interpretation as to imply that all activities which seek to improve health come under the heading of health promotion (Dennis *et al.* 1982). This is at best unhelpful and at worst damaging, in terms of fuzzing the necessary differentiation between powerful, established areas of health service provision and important alternative channels (hitherto seriously neglected) for investment.

In recognition that 'health promotion' had acquired so many meanings as to become meaningless, and taking into account activities undertaken and papers written in the name of health promotion, Tannahill (1985*b*) developed a model for defining, planning, and 'doing' health promotion. This has become widely adopted. The construct can now be described against the essential backdrop of our clarification of the meanings of related terms (Chapters 2 and 3, and pp. 49, 51). According to the Tannahill model (Fig. 4.1), health promotion comprises three overlapping spheres of activity: *health education* (or, more precisely, that part which contributes to the overall goal of health promotion—see p. 25), *prevention* (p. 50), and *health protection* (p. 51).

Seven domains (numbered in the figure) may be distinguished within health promotion, as follows.

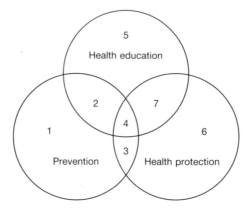

Fig 4.1   A model of health promotion.

1. *Preventive services, etc.* Examples such as immunization and cervical screening have already been touched upon (pp. 50, 56). Hypertension case-finding, screening for handicapping congenital disorders, developmental surveillance, and the use of nicotine-containing chewing gum to aid smoking cessation are other examples.

2. *Preventive health education.* This includes educational efforts to influence lifestyle in the interests of preventing ill-health, as well as efforts to encourage the uptake of preventive services. In addition, the two-way nature of the educational process must not be forgotten: communication channels must be used to ensure that appropriate (wantable) preventive services are provided (see pp. 29, 35, 42).

3. *Preventive health protection.* Numerous examples have already been mentioned (pp. 51–3). Fluoridation of water supplies to prevent dental caries (and possibly also osteoporosis) is another.

4. *Health education for preventive health protection.* One of the most notable successes in this category has been the intensive lobbying for seat-belt legislation (it having been shown that public health education alone was ineffective as a means of securing widespread use of belts in motor vehicles). Efforts to stimulate a social environment conducive to the success of preventive health protection measures are also important here.

[So far, the emphasis has been on prevention. As can be seen from Fig. 4.1, the remaining domains lie outside the sphere of prevention. They are concerned with the enhancement of positive health.]

5. *Positive health education.* As seen in Chapter 3, positive health education falls into two categories: health education aimed at influencing behaviour on positive health grounds (such as the encouragement of a productive use of leisure time in the interests of fitness and well-being); and that which seeks to help individuals, groups, or whole communities to develop positive health attributes (health-related lifeskills and a high level of self-esteem), which are central to the enhancement of true well-being (see p. 19, 42).

6. *Positive health protection.* A positive dimension to health protection has already been mentioned (see p. 51). An example is the implementation of a workplace smoking policy in the interests of providing clean air. Another is the commitment of public funds to the provision of attractive and accessible leisure facilities in order to promote positive health.

7. *Health education aimed at positive health protection.* This involves raising awareness of, and securing support for, positive health protection measures, among the public and policy-makers.

The domains have been presented in this way to demonstrate the wide range of possibilities for health promotion. They are not to be seen as occupying rigidly separate compartments. In particular, it has to be pointed out that the positive and preventive objectives, whether in health education or health protection, will in reality often be combined. The reasons for somewhat artificially separating the two in this account are that the positive dimension is in practice too easily lost and that in fact a good case can often be made for making the positive aim the primary one.

The following summary definition of health promotion arises out of the model presented here. (Note the incorporation of the goal of health promotion as presented at the end of Chapter 2.)

Health promotion comprises efforts to enhance positive health and prevent ill-health, through the overlapping spheres of health education, prevention, and health protection.

The cardinal principle of health promotion thus defined is empowerment. Health education seeks to empower by providing necessary information and helping people to develop skills and a

healthy level of self-esteem (see pp. 30, 35), so that they come to feel
that significant control resides within themselves, rather than feeling buffeted about by external forces outside their sphere of influence. The provision of good preventive services and the shaping of
a healthful environment through health protection also contribute
to this process of empowerment.

4.4 An integrated approach to planning

It will be recalled that Chapter 3 concluded with a discussion of
health education programme planning in the light of philosophical
and organizational principles. We must now broaden out from that
discussion by considering a rational approach to the planning and
delivery of community health promotion programmes, incorporat-
ing health education.

It will be clear from this chapter that we see health education as
the core of health promotion. Accordingly we view health promotion planning as a logical extension of health education planning,
following the same basic principles, namely the need to make two-
way contact with individuals and groups in the community, and the
consequent desirability of selecting community settings and groups,
rather than specific diseases or hazards, as the priorities for action.
Health promotion planning documents to date have often merely
stated the obvious by prioritizing along well-established topic lines,
without adequate attention to methodology. We believe that to do
this is just as simplistic and unnecessary as it would be for a plan for,
say, renal medicine to list a catalogue of relatively common or
important kidney diseases as action priorities without addressing
technique.

We propose an integrated approach to health promotion planning (Fig. 4.2), whereby comprehensive programmes of health
education in key settings and with key groups in the community are
dovetailed with specific preventive services and health protection measures, tailored to the needs of the places and people
concerned.

As implied by Fig 4.2, we suggest that this planning model may be
used at the level of a relatively large community (such as a Scottish
health board area or an English health district), or on the scale of
smaller geographical patches (in keeping with the move in some parts
towards organizing community services on a locality basis). Thus

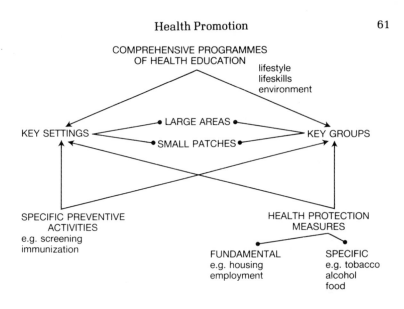

Fig 4.2 An integrated approach to health promotion planning.

area- or district-wide efforts may be made to establish programmes in settings (such as schools) and with groups (for example, old people), while on the smaller scale, professionals and others, working as locally-sensitive teams, can seek to gain access to the various settings and groups in their defined patches. We look on the localization of community services as potentially an extremely exciting and fruitful opportunity for sound health promotion work.

Such community activities will, of course, be complemented by other health education efforts, such as agenda-setting media campaigns, as appropriate (see p. 47), and will be backed by essential larger-scale planning in relation to preventive services (such as screening and immunization) and health protection policies.

4.5 Broader contexts

4.5.1 Health promotion and HFA 2000

At the Thirtieth World Health Assembly in 1977, the attainment of health for all was accepted as the main social target of governments and the World Health Organization in the remaining years of the century. The strategy for 'Health for All by the Year 2000' ('HFA 2000' or 'Health for All') gained momentum with the Declaration of

Alma Ata in 1978, and took further shape in Europe in 1985, with the publication of a book setting out the principles and identifying 38 targets (WHO 1985). The UK Government has expressed strong support for the strategy.

Although the vocabulary used by WHO (WHO 1984) in relation to health promotion and prevention is different from that used in delineating health promotion in this chapter (indeed it is unsatisfactory in a number of respects; Tannahill 1985*b*), it is clear from the HFA 2000 strategy that all aspects of health promotion as defined here are considered to be vital in pursuing better health for everyone. As well as legitimizing health promotion, notably through the 'Ottawa Charter' (WHO 1986), the strategy is centred on certain key principles which are of major relevance to work in this field.

First, as befits a strategy for health for *all*, the promotion of equity in health is a central principle. Health promotion must seek to redress inequalities in health by encouraging equity of opportunity to enjoy good health. Second, the impact on health of policies and services outside the health sector is stressed. This is well seen in the identified *prerequisites for health*, which have major implications for health protection (see pp. 52, 61):

Freedom from the fear of war
Equal opportunity for all
Satisfaction of basic needs
—food
—basic education
—water and sanitation
—decent housing
—secure work and a useful role in society
Political will and public support

Related to this, HFA 2000 emphasizes the need for fruitful intersectoral collaboration. The importance of multidisciplinary collaboration is similarly highlighted. These principles are crucial to health promotion.

Next, community participation in matters affecting their health is an essential feature of the strategy, and of health promotion.

Finally, primary care and health promotion may be seen as 'twin pillars' of the Health for All strategy (Tannahill 1988*a*). It makes good sense to try to strengthen the bridging between these pillars by further developing health promotion in the primary care setting (see p. 89).

4.5.2 Health promotion and public health

Paralleling the growth in interest in health promotion in recent times has been a resurgence of interest in 'public health'. In the course of these developments, rhetoric has often been centred on 'the new public health', no doubt in the recognition of changes in public health challenges with the changing patterns of disease since the famous days of the turn-of-the-century Medical Officer of Health (MOH). This has not always been helpful: there has been a needless division of professional advocacy between health promotion and the new public health when in fact the advocates have generally been talking about the same sorts of measures.

Ideas as to what constitutes public health in the UK have been influenced greatly by the lasting impressions of the period 1948–74, when Medical Officers of Health, employed by local government, were concerned principally with prevention, while public hospital services came under the auspices of hospital boards.

An influential contribution to perceptions of public health was made in 1988, with the publication of 'Public Health in England' (the report of a committee of inquiry chaired by the Chief Medical Officer of the Department of Health, and hence eponymously known as the 'Acheson Report'; DHSS 1988). This document traced the history of public health in the UK and pointed out that immediately prior to 1948 almost all publicly funded preventive activities and health care were under the management of the MOH. It is apparently in returning to this spirit that the Acheson committee arrived at this definition of public health:

the science and art of preventing disease, prolonging life and promoting health through organised efforts of society.

Health promotion as defined in this chapter should thus be treated as a substantial and vital component of public health (Tannahill 1988b).

4.6 Conclusions

1. The customary classification of prevention as 'primary', 'secondary' and 'tertiary' is unsatisfactory.
2. Instead, four foci for prevention may be described, these accommodating notions beyond the mere prevention of disease.

3. Health protection is important in the promotion of positive health and in the prevention of ill-health. Strong action, however, is hampered by powerful vested interests.

4. 'Health promotion' is a highly fashionable term which has, unfortunately, been used in many different ways, often without clarification of meaning.

5. It is helpful, for the purposes of definition, planning, and action, to view health promotion as comprising efforts to enhance positive health and prevent ill-health, through the overlapping spheres of health education, prevention, and health protection. Empowerment is a cardinal principle of health promotion.

6. As with health education, community programmes of health promotion are best planned according to key settings and groups, rather than disease or hazard topics. In each setting and group, a comprehensive programme of health education should be integrated with relevant specific preventive services, etc., and with appropriate health protection measures.

7. Such community programmes should be complemented by appropriate larger-scale efforts in each of the three component spheres of health promotion.

8. Health promotion is a major and integral component of the World Health Organization strategy for 'Health for All by the Year 2000', and of the field of public health.

5 Evaluation

In the previous two chapters we have presented models of health education and health promotion. These models delineate and define our subject area and thereby enable us to identify the activities with which we are legitimately concerned. This is only a start, however. It is necessary to have confidence in the value and effectiveness of the activities—to be able to show that they are worthwhile, that they contribute to the aims of health education and health promotion, and are consistent with the overall philosophy. This requires *evaluation* of the activities.

In this chapter the evaluation process is examined. Our concern is not with the 'how-to-do' of evaluation. Rather, we aim to clarify why we need to evaluate health promotion activities and to examine how we can go about doing so, whilst alerting the reader to the difficulties involved.

5.1 What is evaluation?

Two slightly different views of evaluation pervade the literature on health promotion. From the first viewpoint, evaluation involves assessing an activity in terms of the aims or specific objectives of that activity. For example, Williams (1987; p. 81) has written as follows:

> . . . the purpose of evaluation is that it should demonstrate whether an activity has been successful or to what degree it has failed to achieve some stated aims.

Before we can evaluate, then, we need to be clear about the aims of the activity. We can then judge the value of the activity in relation to the degree of attainment of these aims.

From the second viewpoint, evaluation is a broader process. It involves assessing an activity by measuring it against a standard which is not necessarily related to the specific objectives or purpose of the activity. This approach has been advocated by Green *et al.* (1980; p. 123):

We define evaluation simply as the comparison of an object of interest against a standard of acceptability.

Clearly, as in the first definition, the 'standard of acceptability' may refer to the achievement of aims or objectives. However, this is only one possibility. From this second viewpoint, evaluation may involve assessing an activity according to, for example, the ethics of the approach, the cost of the activity, or the reactions of the recipients or participants.

The first viewpoint may be viewed as a subset of the second. This latter viewpoint is helpful in a number of ways.

First, it is consistent with the fact that we are interested in answering not only the question 'Is the activity effective?', but also questions such as 'At what cost?', 'Using what means?' and 'With what consequences?' In other words, it is a reminder that we cannot be content only with showing that activities are effective at achieving the desired outcome.

Secondly, it clarifies the fact that we should assess the *processes* of health promotion as well as the *outcomes*. When the word 'aims' is used, it is often taken to imply some end-point or goal, and thus has limited and specific connotations. In the following section we advocate a broad interpretation of the term 'aims', to incorporate not only outcomes but also the various procedural aims of health promotion.

Thirdly, it leads us away from a narrow view of suitable outcome measures by alerting us to the presence of a range of standards of acceptability. It follows that a variety of assessment procedures may be appropriately employed in evaluation. The benefits of this are explored in Sections 5.3 and 5.6.

There are some advantages, then, in seeing evaluation in broad rather than specific terms. Nevertheless, evaluation must always be relevant to the aims or objectives of the activity, and the measurements made need to be varied and appropriate. In Section 5.3 we describe some of the measures which may be employed in evaluation. First, however, the terminology will be examined.

5.2 Definition of terms

Whilst there is a general consensus about the way in which many terms are used in discussions of the evaluation of health promotion activities, there seems to be some inconsistency concerning their specific meanings. Our purpose here is to clarify the meanings we attach to them.

The first term which requires definition is *aims*. As in everyday parlance, this term refers to the intention or purpose of an activity. There are three important points to be made about aims:

1. Aims are the planned, or hoped-for, effects of an activity.
2. Aims tend to be general, and may be broken down into specific *objectives*, each of which contributes in some way to its associated aim.
3. Aims may concern the long-or short-term consequences of a programme, or may refer to some aspect of the process of programme implementation or operation.

This final point requires some clarification.

Activities in the field of health promotion may be examined in three broad stages. The initial stage involves planning and design; the second, the 'running' of the programme; and the third, observing the effects. Whilst one of the reasons for evaluating programmes is to enable improvements in their design, the process of evaluation is generally concerned with assessing the second and third stages of the activity of interest. Terms are therefore required to refer to these post-design phases.

The implementation and 'maintenance' of a programme is called the *process*. It involves all the workings of the programme, its different components, and their interactions. Clearly, this machinery has to be in order before any programme can be expected to work as planned. Evaluation of process is an essential step towards achieving the desired effects from a programme.

The effects, or consequences, of a programme may be observed (if they exist) at any stage over a period of time after exposure to, or implementation of, the programme. For convenience we may distinguish between those consequences observed more or less immediately and those resulting after a longer period of time. Henceforth we shall refer to the former as *impact* and to the latter as *outcome*.

In evaluating a programme, we may be interested in any or all of the three facets—process, impact, and outcome—and we need measures of each. Collectively these can be termed *output measures*. In this sense, output refers to manufacture as well as yield, as it includes aspects of the programme process as well as the effects. This clearly differs from common epidemiological interpretations of the term, as for example: 'The immediate result of professional or institutional health care activities, usually expressed as units of service, e.g. patient hospital days, outpatient visits, laboratory tests performed' (Last 1988).

To summarize, the evaluation of a programme involves assessing it in relation to its aims or its (more specific) objectives. The aims and objectives refer to the hopes for the programme, both in terms of the way in which it operates or runs, and also in terms of its short- and long-term effects. These concerns—the subjects of the aims and objectives—are respectively termed process, impact, and outcome. Together they constitute the programme output. There are many measures of output which are relevant in the evaluation of health promotion programmes. These are outlined in the following section.

5.3 Measures of output

The previous discussions have emphasized that evaluation must always be relevant to the aims of the activity being assessed, and these aims should be explicitly stated. It follows that the output measures (measurements of the process, of the immediate impact of activities, and of the long-term outcome) must also be appropriate to the aims. Measurements of individual behaviour will not always do. For example, sometimes the interest lies with economic measures, or educational measures, or assessment of change in social attitudes or in environmental conditions. We thus need a variety of appropriate measures of output.

In addition to being appropriate, the measures must meet the criteria of repeatability and validity. Repeatability refers to the extent to which a measurement gives the same answer when the subject is re-examined. Provided that there is no relevant change in the subject or conditions of assessment, a repeatable measure will yield consistent responses every time it is applied. Validity refers to the extent to which a measurement actually does measure what it purports to measure. The validity of a measurement may be tested by comparing it with another, accepted measure.

Figure 5.1 indicates a broad aim for health promotion (derived from Chapter 2), some of the associated objectives, and output measures which could appropriately be used in the evaluation of activities. Clearly, each measure has its own relatively specific use. Health promotion involves a wide range of diverse activities, and its evaluation is problematic for the many reasons described in Section

5.5, but there is a range of output measures and methods which can appropriately be used to evaluate the effects of activities.

Aim	Measure
To prevent ill-health while promoting positive health	Health indicators

Objectives	Measures/Methods
To change knowledge and beliefs	Health knowledge Perceived risks
To change attitudes and values (inc. self-awareness & self-esteem)	Values-clarification Attitude scales (e.g. Likert scale) Lawseq self-esteem scale*
To enhance decision-making skills	Assessment of behaviour
To change behaviour	Assessment of behaviour
To establish health promoting environments	Environmental monitoring Policies in public places
To achieve healthful social change	Surveys of social attitudes/values
To foster empowerment of individuals and communities	Locus of control (e.g. MHLC scales**) Assessment of behaviour
To achieve the above in optimal and acceptable ways	Efficiency Cost effectiveness/cost benefit ratio Ethical assessment

* Lawrence (1981)
** Wallston and Wallston (1978)

Fig 5.1   A guide to health promotion evaluation

The list in this figure is not wholly comprehensive but highlights those measures which are most frequently used. It is beyond the scope of this discussion to examine each in turn so we shall concentrate on some general points in relation to the measurement of positive health and ill-health.

Levels of health in individuals and in populations have conventionally been measured using *objective* indices, such as biochemical, microbiological, and radiological tests, blood pressure measurement, and behavioural assessment, in the first instance; and mortality, morbidity, and service utilization (e.g. bed occupancy) rates, in the second. However, it has become noted increasingly that these measures are not appropriate measures of the *health* of individuals and populations, in the complete sense of health as described in Chapter 2. There are several reasons for this:

1. In general they are measures of illness and disease, and make no contribution to the measurement of positive health.
2. They are principally measures of the physical component of health and neglect the important mental and social aspects.
3. They are based on professional assessments and professional opinions of the crucial components of health. They therefore take little or no account of lay perceptions of health and lay priorities for health.

These objective measurements have thus been found to give misleading impressions about health. For example, a decreasing mortality rate does not necessarily mean an increasingly healthy population, just as the absence of abnormality in biochemical or radiological tests does not mean that the individual being assessed is healthy. For all these reasons it has become clear that more sophisticated indices are required to measure health status.

As outlined in Chapter 2, health may be assessed in terms of a set of properties, attributes, or characteristics. It is this approach that has been pursued by researchers involved in developing *subjective* indicators of health. These indicators measure health in terms of an eclectic set of 'characteristics' of individuals—functional capacity, pain, social activity, physical mobility, and so on. This approach is consistent with the various other conceptions of health: it includes the perspectives of social health and positive health; it incorporates the medical model of health as the absence of disease; and it emphasizes the experiential concept of feeling ill (or well), whether or not disease is present.

There are two types of health indicator: the health profile and the health index.

Health profiles provide a descriptive account of different aspects of health (such as pain, physical mobility, social life, etc.). Each of these aspects is described in quantitative terms, but the disparate measurements are not aggregated. Thereby a profile quantifying different aspects of health is yielded. The Nottingham Health Profile is a good example (see Hunt, *et al.* 1986).

Health indices go a step further than the profiles, by aggregating measurements of many different aspects of performance and experience into a single value. For example, the Index of Health (Chiang 1965; Chiang and Cohen 1973) is a measure of the health of a population. It is calculated from the expected total duration of illness in the population during a year, weighted for age structure, and incorporates an adjustment for deaths and (in its later form) a factor for severity of illness. It aggregates the values from these various components on to a single scale.

Another type of single global indicator which has been developed and widely acknowledged is the 'Quality-adjusted life year' or QALY. QALYs may be used to combine quality and duration of survival in the assessment of programmes or services. This is more sensitive than the traditional measure of 'life expectancy', since acknowledgement is made of the fact that some activities may improve the quality of life whilst having no effect on its duration, and others may prolong life but have a detrimental effect on its quality (Williams 1983). QALYs have been most widely used by health economists and those interested in comparing different health care services. They are useful tools for decisions about the allocation of resources, but reservations have been expressed not only about the methodology of their derivation but also concerning their use as an 'automatic decision-making device' replacing political discussion and management judgements (Smith 1987).

Clearly the choice of which health indicator to employ will depend on the purpose for which it is being used. Within the field of health promotion, however, the profile approach is seen to have several advantages over the global health index.

First, the aggregation of different components into a single index inevitably results in the loss of information. Given the range of objectives of health promotion activities, it follows that the output measures should involve assessments of the various components of health rather than the reduction of information to a single value.

Secondly, whilst the development of a valid and reliable health profile is far from straightforward, it avoids many of the methodological difficulties inherent in the construction of indices, such as the problem of combining like with unlike, and of assuming that some factors inevitably add more to the state of health than do others.

Thirdly, whereas the index approach is most useful for the assessment of outcome of different interventions, or for comparing the effects of different health care services, health profiles provide more appropriate measures of the state of health of individuals and populations. They too can be used to compare the relative situations of individuals or groups, but this is not their sole purpose. The needs of health promotion, similarly, are more often concerned with detailed assessment of the state of health within a population of interest than with comparing this population to another.

Health indicators may be based on subjective perceptions (judgements made by the person whose health is being measured) or on objective assessment, usually by a health professional. Although objective measurements are usually of the index type, the subjective/objective distinction does not exactly correspond to the profile/index dichotomy. Historically, objective measures have been preferred as they have been viewed as more valid, being made by those with expertise in 'health', and more reliable, because they use techniques which measure something absolute, and are not dependent on someone's belief and opinion. These assumptions have now all been questioned, and subjective measures such as the Nottingham Health Profile have been found to be valid, repeatable and, for our purposes, more appropriate measures of health.

There are several reasons why subjective indicators are of value to those involved with health promotion activities.

1. It is *perceived*, not necessarily *actual* situations which result in the adoption of health-related behaviours, including the demand for health care. For example, people who are dependent on alcohol may make artificial assessments of their position and of the effects of their drinking habits. As long as they do not perceive the existence of a problem they will not seek help, whether or not an objective assessment of their physical, mental, and social health indicates that they are in a poor state. The subjective indicator of health is a better predictor of behaviour than is the objective measure.

2. Because health promotion involves two-way communication and a 'bottom-up' approach, it is crucial for workers to be aware of, and to understand, the health beliefs and perceptions of the subjects with whom they are working. Only then can programmes be made appropriate and relevant to perceived needs. Moreover, activities which recognize lay beliefs will be more effective as they can tackle issues which are perceived as 'real', in a language known to their clients.

3. Subjective indicators are not restricted by professionally defined scales or terminologies. Instead they are based upon lay people's own assessments and personal valuation systems. This is clearly more appropriate for health promotion, which looks beyond the medical model of health and is aiming to affect lay beliefs about health.

Subjective assessments of health are consistent with the overall philosophy of health promotion and they are not restricted by any one professional model of health. They are good predictors of behaviour, and provide an essential foundation for effective planning and communication about health-related issues.

5.4 Why evaluate?

There are five main reasons for evaluating health promotion programmes.

1. *To ensure that activities are having the desired effect.* Without evaluation we cannot know what influence the initiatives have had. Have they had any effect? If so, has the effect been in the desired direction? Knowledge of the effect can be used constructively to improve activities, and to reinforce those that are valuable and worthwhile.

2. *To minimize waste of resources.* Without evaluation we cannot tell if good use is being made of the finite amounts of time and money available for health promotion. Clearly, cost cutting must not be the only criterion for success of initiatives. If it were, the most successful initiatives would be those ensuring the death of people once they reached pensionable age (see p. 53). On the other hand, those involved in health promotion are accountable both to the public and to funding bodies for the resources used.

3. *To improve materials and methods.* Activities may be having a

favourable effect (or at least not a detrimental effect), but often they could be doing better. The desired outcome might be achieved, but by sub-optimal means. Without evaluation we cannot compare different approaches or assess new innovations.

4. *To assess the validity of scepticism about the effectiveness of health promotion.* Health promotion is a relatively new area of expertise and as such is exposed to greater degrees of suspicion and opposition than are more established fields and professions. We need to assess the validity of this scepticism and be able to counter it where appropriate. Sometimes we can provide assurance on the basis of prior research, but in many cases there have been no appropriate previous studies, and so new evaluation studies are often necessary.

5. *To assess whether activities are ethically justifiable.* By definition, health promotion initiatives aim to affect people's lives in a healthful manner. In doing so they may cause some inconvenience or discomfort. Are such effects justifiable? Do the results of the health promotion activities warrant the personal expense, time, and intrusion into people's lives which they may incur? Only by evaluating the activities can we assess whether the effects of a particular approach are justifiable.

For all these reasons it is important to evaluate health promotion programmes. Once again, though, there should be a word or two of caution. Evaluation itself costs money: this is especially significant given the chronic underfunding of health promotion initiatives. Moreover, evaluation too may intrude into people's lives and cost them time and effort; it may involve them in the completion of questionnaires, which may be time-consuming and stressful, and in the provision of information which may be sensitive or personal. Often there is no feedback to these participants, and if there is it may be meaningless or incomprehensible to them. Is the inconvenience of the evaluation procedure justifiable?

Both of these difficulties can be dealt with and remedied to a certain extent (Ledwith 1986), and they certainly do not undermine the many advantages that may accrue from evaluation studies. The point is simply that just as health promotion activities should not be carried out at any cost, neither should evaluation be carried out at any cost.

5.5 Issues in evaluation

The evaluation of health promotion initiatives is far from straight-forward. Indeed there are difficulties to be encountered at all stages of the evaluation process, from its planning through its execution to the final stage of making recommendations. Two valuable papers (Green 1977; Baric 1980) have discussed difficulties relating to the evaluation of health education. These are, of course, of central relevance to the larger field of health promotion, and so the following discussion incorporates many of the issues identified by those two authors.

5.5.1 The difficulty of isolating the effects of a specific health promotion programme

Within the field of health promotion there is often a variety of initiatives involving the same community, which aim to influence the same health factors and effect the same healthful change. The problem, then, is to isolate the effects resulting specifically from one of these initiatives. Similarly, in observing a trend in a given index it is problematical to relate this trend with certainty to a given health promotion input. For example, in the UK we have been observing a decline over the last 40 years in the prevalence of cigarette smoking among the adult male population. How can we assess the relative contributions of health education, legislative, and fiscal measures to this trend?

5.5.2 The difficulty of integrating different approaches to evaluation

It follows from our broad interpretation of the evaluation process—as the assessment of activities in a variety of ways against a variety of standards—that a range of approaches to evaluation should be adopted. Moreover, workers from a variety of backgrounds may be involved in the evaluation process and in the interpretation of the results. There is thus a problem of integrating the range of expertise and the various approaches which arise from this multidisciplinary activity. Recently, however, there has been some progress towards the integration of different approaches. Everly *et al.* (1987), for example, have examined ways of integrating behavioural and financial models in the evaluation of health promotion programmes in the workplace, to answer simultaneously the two questions, 'Does the programme work?' and 'At what cost?'

A necessary step towards integrating approaches is the acceptance of standardized procedures and terminology for evaluation. Green and Lewis (1987) have proposed standardization of this type for the evaluation of health education. However, we are a long way from having standard, accepted terminology and procedures for evaluation within and across all the domains of health promotion—and this acts as a barrier to effective and appropriate evaluation.

5.5.3 Evaluation must be appropriate to the stage of service development

Within the health (and other) services, health promotion is still at a relatively early stage of development. Evaluators must therefore be careful to avoid making demands inappropriate to the stage of service development, or else the results of evaluation will inevitably be discouraging. Once again we see the clear need for evaluation of *processes*, particularly in relation to the development of new initiatives. Only once health promotion services are properly primed can we realistically expect them to be effective at achieving the desired impact or outcome.

5.5.4 Lack of clearly-defined objectives

While in many health services the aim of an activity is specific—to improve visual acuity, to destroy malignant cells, or to treat dental caries, for example—within health promotion the aim is often seen as the more general one of preventing ill-health and simultaneously enhancing positive health. Now, unless an activity has one or more *specific objectives*, by achievement of which it will contribute to the attainment of this overall aim, it cannot be evaluated. It is imperative that these objectives be made explicit at the planning stage and that evaluation is relative to these stated objectives.

5.5.5 Resistance to review and assessment

It is often the case that those who evaluate programmes are not those who are actually carrying out health promotion initiatives. This situation has one clear benefit in that the evaluators are likely to have a certain amount of objectivity: their lack of personal involvement with the specific service being evaluated may well free them from potential sources of subjective bias. However, those involved in carrying out health promotion may exhibit some resistance to review and assessment—especially when this is made by someone without specialist health promotion expertise who is thus unaware of many of the issues in its practice.

5.5.6 Political and vested interests

Political factors affect the evaluation of health promotion in a number of ways. They determine which programmes and policies exist in the first place, through both resourcing and other influences. Resource levels in turn affect the scope for evaluation. Furthermore, reports and recommendations from evaluation exercises have to compete for attention and implementation with other calls for political commitment.

In other words, politics influence *what* can be evaluated, *how* it is evaluated, and the *whether* and *when* of recommendations being adopted.

5.5.7 Time factors

There is a problem of when to evaluate, as the outcome of an activity will vary at different time periods after the intervention. Some effects of health promotion are immediate whilst others are slow in emerging. Some effects are transient and others longer lasting. In the absence of prohibitively expensive and time-consuming longitudinal studies, various time-related problems in evaluation have to be recognized. These have been described as 'the dilemma of long vs. short-term evaluation', and categorized as follows (Green 1977):

1. *Delay of impact.* This occurs, for example, when a process of attitude change has to be undertaken before behaviour change can take place. If we evaluate too soon after the intervention, then the behaviour change will not be observed.

2. *Decay of impact.* In some cases the intervention will have a more or less immediate effect which decreases over time. If we evaluate too late we will not measure the immediate impact; and if we do observe an effect we cannot assume it to be permanent.

3. *Borrowing from the future.* Sometimes interventions merely hasten behavioural change, such as smoking cessation, that

would have occurred anyway. This may, of course, have real benefits, but we have to be careful not to overestimate the effects of an intervention.

4. *Adjusting for secular trends.* If the objective of an intervention is to increase the prevalence of a variable, and if this variable is on the increase anyway and we fail to adjust for this, we shall overestimate the benefits of the intervention. If the general trend is a decline in the variable of interest, then the benefit of the intervention may be underestimated.

5. *Contrast effect.* This may occur when a programme is terminated prematurely, or when the subjects have expectations which are not fulfilled. A consequently embittered group of 'clients' may act in defiance of advice on behaviour, producing a 'backlash effect'. Evaluation during, or soon after, the intervention would measure the benefits but not the contrasting backlash which occurred after termination of the activity.

5.5.8 Absence of experimental conditions

Scientific experiments demand rigorous conditions, standardization of environments, and precision of procedure. For the evaluation of health promotion programmes working with communities, however, conditions such as these will not be present. Moreover, we should not insist on total experimental rigour in situations where it is not justified. Health promotion programmes should not be restricted by the demands of evaluators to 'carry out the original plan no matter what', but rather should be allowed to develop to their full potential taking advantage of the expertise and initiative of those implementing them.

5.6 Approaches to evaluation

So far we have discussed the evaluation process only in general terms, as if the term 'evaluation' itself is an adequate explanation of what is being done. The process is much more complicated than that, however, and any of a variety of approaches to evaluation may be adopted. When describing an evaluation study it is important to provide answers to the following questions at least:

— *When* was the evaluation carried out?
— *What* was evaluated?
— *Why* was the evaluation carried out?
— *How* was the evaluation carried out?

5.6.1 When was the evaluation carried out?

Evaluation studies which are carried out while the programme of interest is still happening are known as *formative* evaluations, and those which take place after it is ended are called *summative* evaluations. Clearly, as was illustrated by the seat-belt legislation in the UK, attitudes and behaviour are often found to change after a policy is established. Thus attitudes detected during a formative evaluation might not correspond to those identified by a summative evaluation. Both approaches are valuable.

5.6.2 What was evaluated?

Approaches to evaluation may be classified according to the particular aspect of the programme which is to be evaluated: *process*, *impact*, or *outcome* (as defined earlier on p. 67). Health promotion programmes are commonly evaluated in terms of impact. Evaluation of this type is relatively easy and inexpensive to carry out; and it helps to provide an answer to the question of whether the programme 'works' in the short-term.

In Section 5.5.3, however, we stressed that there should be caution about over-emphasis on evaluating the impact of programmes, and we argued for the importance of process evaluation. Although health professionals may be resistant to critical review of their skills and procedures, this must not act as a barrier to process evaluation.

Outcome evaluation addresses the question: 'Does it work in the long-term?' It is important to distinguish between 'ultimate' outcome (in terms of health status) and other outcomes (such as cognitive or behavioural outcomes) more directly related to a programme's stated objectives. Often it is the latter type which is appropriate for gauging the effects of an intervention.

5.6.3 Why was the evaluation carried out?

In Section 5.4 we listed five main reasons for evaluating health promotion activities. In addition to carrying out evaluation of a health promotion programme for any of these specific reasons, it is possible to classify different approaches to evaluation. The classification adopted here is based upon the four types of evaluation proposed by Arnold (1972).

Firstly, assessment may be made of the health promotion programme as a complete system, examining the relative needs and contributions of its component parts. It is most important that the programme should be functional as a whole, with each component being primed to a level sufficient for the attainment of its objectives.

Secondly, particular strategies may be evaluated to assess their relative effectiveness and ethical acceptability.

Thirdly, the management of the programme may be evaluated to examine how it works in practice, comparing this to its proposed effectiveness at the planning stage. Evaluation can assess the extent and effects of any changes that have occurred from planning to implementation.

Finally, we might carry out relevance evaluation, to ensure that the initiatives are up-to-date and appropriate. Health promotion programmes which are outdated, or which neglect pertinent new information or issues, are likely to be sub-optimal, and indeed may actually cause harm.

5.6.4 How was the evaluation carried out?

The decision about how to evaluate is often determined by the availability of resources, and by the feasibility of different evaluative designs. The evaluation of health promotion programmes owes much to epidemiological method, and various designs are available.

Basic evaluation can be carried out simply by record-keeping. For example, routine data collected about attendance at outpatient clinics will indicate fluctuations which may be associated with relevant health promotion initiatives and provide an indication of their impact.

Simple evaluation by observing trends over time does not permit us to conclude whether these trends result from health promotion activities or whether they would have occurred anyway. One way of clarifying this is to make a comparison with a comparable location where the intervention of interest is absent. This is known as a controlled-comparison (quasi-experimental) approach. Another comparative design involves comparing the situation of interest with others where there is a similar intervention.

In the comparative designs described above, comparison groups fall outside the sphere of influence of the evaluation exercise. Another approach is to have an experimental design similar to that used in a clinical trial. This is a controlled-experimental approach. Subjects (or collections of subjects) are randomly assigned to an intervention group or a control group. A more complex approach along the same lines of design involves more than two groups, exposed to different 'doses' of intervention.

Clearly these experimental approaches have limited application for the evaluation of many health promotion initiatives. Sometimes they would be unethical: how could we justify withholding education about health services, for example, from a group of the population? In other circumstances they might be infeasible: for instance, how could a group of the population be made exempt from legislative or fiscal measures? Moreover, except in certain specific circumstances, such as the use of preventive medication, the 'double-blind' ideal of the clinical trial cannot be achieved in health promotion evaluation: there is, for example, no placebo for a health education intervention. Thus, whilst this controlled-experimental design is the most desirable epidemiologically, its applicability to the evaluation of health promotion practice is limited.

The evaluation of health promotion programmes must be carried out in the field, in the settings in which the programmes are taking place. We cannot expect to achieve laboratory conditions, and we should not expect to. This point is made clear by Green *et al.* (1980; p. 140):

The problem with the more complicated designs is that they usually have to be carried out under highly controlled conditions, which makes behavioural circumstances unusual or unnatural . . . what one gains in neutral validity through the more rigorous randomised procedures one may sacrifice in feasibility and generalizability of findings.

Often, the quasi-experimental approach will be found to be the most appropriate and acceptable.

5.7 Conclusions

1. We advocate a broad definition of evaluation, involving a range of approaches and output measures.

2. Evaluation of health promotion activities must be relevant to the aims of these activities. Appropriate aims are diverse and include many objectives in addition to the traditional educational ones of changing beliefs, attitudes, and behaviour.

3. We have identified the main reasons for evaluating health promotion programmes. In summary, we need to ascertain the effects of programmes, assess the methods employed, and examine the use of resources.

4. It is essential not to expect from health promotion activities results inappropriate to the stage of service development. Over ambitious demands will inevitably be frustrated. At early stages of development there should be strong emphasis on evaluating the *process* of health promotion.

5. The methodology employed for evaluation should not be so epidemiologically rigorous as to inhibit initiative and development in the field. The evaluation of health promotion programmes must be carried out in the settings in which the programmes are taking place, and it is inappropriate to expect to achieve laboratory conditions.

6 Models in action

The purpose of this chapter is to demonstrate, through selected examples, how the various models presented so far may be translated into practice. We shall start by considering an actual case study in health *education*, to do with a topic-based response to a new health hazard (snuff-dipping products). We shall then look in some detail at the applicability of the model of health *promotion* (see Chapter 4), in turn, to a disease topic (coronary heart disease), a risk factor topic (alcohol), and two key community settings (primary health care and schools).

6.1 Health education and a risk factor topic

With reference to the model of health promotion (Fig. 6.1), this case study is an example of health education for preventive health protection (the domain labelled number 4 in the figure). That is to say, the initiative which will now be described represents an attempt to secure, through education, preventive regulatory action against a specific health hazard.

6.1.1 The problem

In Scotland, in 1985, health professionals, politicians, trades unionists, Action on Smoking and Health (ASH), the media, and parents of young children joined forces in protest against 'Skoal Bandits'. US Tobacco Inc. had opened a factory in East Kilbride to manufacture these products, little teabag-like sachets containing moist tobacco, designed to be placed in the mouth between cheek and gum (a practice known as 'snuff-dipping').

Disquiet about these and other snuff-dipping products (SDPs) centred mainly around the facts that they had been shown to contain known carcinogens (Harrison 1986), that they had been linked to cancer of the mouth in the United States (Winn *et al.* 1981; USNIH 1986), and that an expert committee had declared this asso-

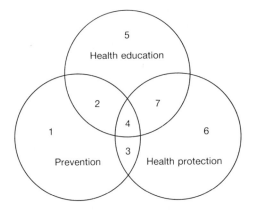

Fig 6.1   The model of health promotion.

ciation to be causal (DHSS 1985). In addition, snuff-dipping has been implicated in lesser mouth problems, such as recession of the gums. The problems are magnified by the likelihood of nicotine dependence, and widened out by the attendant possibility of 'graduation' to smoking.

Concern was focused largely on young people: in the United States snuff-dipping had become very popular with youngsters, especially boys, encouraged by general product imagery (such as the masked bandit logo of Skoal Bandits and the association of SDPs with baseball heroes through advertising), and promotional ploys (including the giving out of free samples at rodeos). In the UK the style of promotion had disregarded the spirit of the voluntary agreement not to encourage the use of SDPs by young people.

A strong element of outrage was added to the public protest by reports that a Government Department had contributed around £1 million of public funds towards US Tobacco's East Kilbride venture (Cameron 1985). A tinge of farce was contributed by the fact that the Government's Health Departments were so concerned about snuff-dipping that letters were sent to all doctors and dentists warning them about the dangers of the practice and discouraging the use of the products.

This case study is concerned with the response to snuff-dipping in one English Health Region—East Anglia. In late 1985, following media coverage of the Scottish campaign against SDPs, the East Anglian Regional Health Promotion Group (EARHPG) set up a small task group to monitor the situation locally and devise action as appropriate. (EARHPG is a body set up by the Regional Health Authority but including representatives from various agencies outside the health service.) Over the next few months several low-key tasks were undertaken, including the provision of information to health and local authority officers, community health councils, and Members of Parliament throughout the region.

Action had to be stepped up in mid-1986, following reports that SDPs were being promoted and sold in East Anglia.

6.1.2 Options for action

EARHPG considered a proposal for a region-wide media campaign in support of a public petition for a national ban on SDPs. This was rejected. At the time there was much to suggest from official attitudes and actions that a ban would not be forthcoming: without this outcome the exercise might have backfired by stimulating interest in, and thus demand for, products which were as yet not widely available. The risk of inadvertent promotion of SDPs similarly ruled out other high-profile options (such as the production of an education package for schools).

Instead, a low-profile initiative, led by the Regional Health Promotion Officer, was decided upon. The principal aim of this was to discourage potential retailers from promoting or selling SDPs.

6.1.3 The retailers' initiative

The Regional Health Promotion Officer asked the 20 local authority environmental health departments in the region to provide names and addresses of potential retailers of SDPs. Each identified retail outlet was sent a locally produced leaflet which gave information about the products and their dangers, and outlined action already taken in the UK and abroad. An accompanying letter drew particular attention to the EARHPG's concern that children were especially vulnerable, and invited retailers to sign and return (by Freepost) a tear-off slip, thereby pledging not to promote or sell SDPs. The campaign was launched with a press release which emphasized the low-key nature of the project and stressed the need to avoid potentially counterproductive publicity. A follow-up mailing of the campaign materials was undertaken some four months after the launch.

6.1.4 Results

Two thousand, four hundred potential retail outlets were success-fully contacted. By the end of the campaign, 1309 signed pledges had been received (797 in the first phase, 512 in the second).

In addition, 'bottom-up' action by retailers resulted in eight major national/sub-national chains pledging not to promote or sell SDPs in any of their stores.

6.1.5 Discussion

The campaign represents an appropriate and effective (topic-based —see p. 47) response to a new health hazard. It is clearly preferable to block such hazards at source than to depend on public health education once they have become established. Furthermore, the campaign was successful in its important objective of avoiding unwanted publicity, thanks to good relationships with local media. Another notable feature was the fruitful collaboration between health service staff, local authority officers, and others.

The project demonstrates how, in the absence of strong national regulation, health education involving crucial power-holders can result in local preventive health protection measures and can directly stimulate action far beyond the locality in question. Also, it is to be hoped that a local initiative of this type, coupled with activities elsewhere, can contribute to a climate in which legislation is more likely. Certainly in 1990, following wide consultation, UK Health Ministers decided to ban SDPs under the Consumer Protection Act, 1987.

6.2 Health promotion and a disease topic

Not surprisingly, much effort has been devoted in the UK towards devising strategies for health promotion aimed at the prevention of coronary heart disease (CHD), the nation's largest single cause of death. We shall now use the health promotion model (Fig. 6.1) as a planning tool for CHD prevention, referring to the domains of activity as numbered in the figure.

1. Preventive activities relating to CHD include hypertension case-finding, the provision of nicotine-containing chewing gum to aid smoking cessation, and the effective management of

predisposing conditions (such as diabetes mellitus and hypothyroidism).

The role of mass blood cholesterol 'screening' has been the subject of considerable controversy in recent times. We shall not go into the opposing views in any depth here. We shall simply report that an expert panel has concluded that 'mass measurement of blood cholesterol levels in the population is not justified' (King Edward's Hospital Fund for London 1989). There is, however, a consensus in favour of blood cholesterol testing for selected individuals (such as people with a family history of 'premature' CHD, and people with known predisposing conditions).

2. This domain includes health education aimed at influencing lifestyle on the grounds of CHD prevention (important risk factors being smoking, certain aspects of diet, and lack of exercise), and that which encourages the uptake of any relevant preventive service (see domain 1 above).

3. Apposite preventive health protection measures would include those concerned with fundamental health determinants relevant to CHD (such as socio-economic disadvantage), and those aimed at specific risk factors (for example, fiscal action on tobacco—see p. 52, the control of tobacco advertising and promotion, and other policies on tobacco, food, and exercise in the workplace and elsewhere).

4. This involves educational efforts to secure appropriate preventive health protection measures (see domain 3 above).

   [We now come to consider the place of *positive* aspects of health promotion in relation to CHD, which are often neglected as a result of the essentially negative nature of preventive programmes.]

5. Both aspects of this domain of positive health education—that concerned with encouraging certain behaviours on positive health grounds, and that aimed at developing positive health attributes (see p. 59)—are highly relevant to the promotion of lifestyles which protect against CHD.

6. Similarly, the health protection measures for CHD prevention have additional positive benefits (for instance, policies on smoking positively improve the physical environment—see p. 59), and this should be reflected in the advocacy of such regulations and policies.

6.3 Health promotion and a risk factor topic

There is much concern over the growing problems associated with the use of alcohol. These include physical, mental, and social effects, not only on drinkers themselves but also on their families and society at large. Once again the health promotion model (Fig. 6.1) may be used to explore possibilities for action, as follows.

1. Preventive provision in this context would include measures designed to detect problem drinking or its deleterious affects as early as possible, and self-help groups and other agencies aimed at reducing the impact of alcohol problems.

2. Once again there is a place for preventive health education—to discourage situational, acute, or chronic misuse of alcohol on risk-reduction grounds, and to encourage the use of preventive services (see domain 1 above).

3. Preventive health protection would include fundamental aspects of public policy (in recognition of the links between social pressures and the use of drugs of solace). Specific legislation might address the sale of alcohol (for example, regulations concerning age or more general questions of accessibility to alcohol—for instance, through supermarkets), its advertising and promotion, or its consumption (for example, in football grounds and other public places). The desirability of regular increases in duty has already been discussed (see p. 52). In recent times there has also been an upsurge of interest in devising and implementing workplace alcohol policies.

4. Once more, education is necessary to encourage preventive health protection.

5. Education concerning alcohol need not, and should not, be confined to *preventive* considerations. It is important (in schools for example) to employ approaches to health education which encourage people to look at alcohol—its responsible and irresponsible use—in relation to subjective well-being and more objective measures of performance, rather than merely painting alcohol as 'a bad thing'. In doing this, we can try to stimulate a culture more favourable to the consumption of non-alcoholic and low-alcohol drinks. We can also promote ways of using leisure time other than by drinking. Moreover, as with the CHD example, the fostering of positive health attributes is of crucial

relevance to alcohol. We should be developing and evaluating work on assertiveness and stress management training in relation to alcohol use, and we should be trying to foster self-esteem and nurture decision-making skills.

6. Likewise, positive objectives should be incorporated into alcohol-related health protection efforts. The use of alcohol-free and low-alcohol alternatives could be encouraged by regulations on differential pricing (comparable to those to do with unleaded petrol), and by policies favouring their promotion in an attractive manner (reinforcing the educational efforts outlined under domain 5 above). We could look at ways in which we could improve the environment of licensed premises in such a way as to promote the responsible use of alcohol and the freedom (actual and perceived) to choose non-alcoholic drinks. Policies which lead to the provision of attractive and accessible leisure facilities as an alternative to bars would also be worthy of attention.

7. Health education efforts must be directed at securing measures of the sort described under domain 6 above.

6.4 Health promotion and a key setting— primary health care

The examples presented as Sections 6.2 and 6.3 serve to illustrate that the health promotion model can be readily applied to disease and risk factor topics. In the course of these illustrations, important areas of commonality in the area of positive health education will, however, have been noted (see also p. 42). Indeed, in considering health education in relation to CHD—both preventive and positive in orientation—we have seen that the aspects of lifestyle, lifeskills and environment to be addressed are of great relevance to other aspects of (negative and positive) health. These observations in practical examples reinforce our earlier endorsement of planning and prioritizing health education and health promotion programmes in communities primarily according to *people* and *places* rather than *problems* (see pp. 46, 60).

In keeping with this advocacy, we shall conclude this chapter by considering health promotion in two key settings, starting with primary health care. The importance of health promotion in this setting is reflected in the 1990 contract for general medical practitioners (Chisholm 1990). The reader should bear in mind key principles of health education (pp. 35-7) and in particular professional—client communication (p. 43).

1. The primary health care team can provide or participate in the full range of preventive health services (see p. 58), and can facilitate the development of other preventive activities (such as particular types of self-help groups).

2. Education—opportunistic or more structured (for example, based on routine health checks), with individuals or with groups —can be used towards the prevention of the full range of ill-health associated with lifestyle. The simple matter of advising someone to stop smoking, in the course of a consultation, may in favourable circumstances trigger action (Russell *et al.* 1979). Preventive services provided by the primary care team, in other health service settings, and by other agencies (such as social services), as well as other preventive activities (arising from community development work, perhaps), may be promoted through health education. Leaflets may be used not only to amplify verbal advice or instructions but also to encourage the uptake of preventive services in this way. It is important for the primary care team to ascertain, and link in with, the range of formally and informally provided initiatives in their local community. Links with the community, in the spirit of two-way education, may be built up through the establishment of patient participation groups.

3. Health protection policies, such as non-smoking policies, can be created for primary care premises.

4. Members of the team can play an active part, both as individuals and as groups (for example,through their own professional organizations or networks), in encouraging local and national policies to protect against ill-health. Primary care professionals have an important advocacy role, and indeed may view themselves as something akin to health MPs—'political' representatives of their practice lists in the face of threats to health, such as poor housing, unemployment, poverty, or dangerous industrial processes.

5. Health education in primary care must take on board the importance of positive health as a motivation for behaviour change. For too long health professionals have recommended alterations in lifestyles in an off-putting manner—reinforcing perceptions that a healthful lifestyle has to be dull, painful, self-sacrificing,

or otherwise unpleasant—rather than painting positive images. Also, efforts must be made to use consultations and other contacts to help the development of the positive health attributes referred to repeatedly in this chapter and elsewhere. A very basic example of recognizing the importance of skills rather than simply information would be to facilitate dietary modification by providing straightforward recipes instead of merely giving advice to reduce fats, increase fibre, and so on.

6. Health protection policies for the primary care setting will once again have positive aspects (for example, the clean air benefits of a non-smoking policy).

7. In fulfilling their potential role as health protection advocates, primary care professionals should remember also the positive quality of health protection measures beyond their premises (for instance, by pressing for decent local leisure facilities in the interests of positive health—well-being and fitness).

The repeated reference above to the primary care *team* is important. Proper teamwork requires a power balance distinct from that implicit in models of *delegation* from the doctor to others. It involves recognition and appropriate utilization of team member's skills, and the earning, and granting, of mutual professional respect. It will be clear from the above account that specific inputs on diseases and risk factors are essential. We have never denied this (see p. 47). Our argument is simply that we need to develop programmes, in primary care and elsewhere, in a *co-ordinated* manner, bringing together the interlinking strands of preventive and positive health education in a participatory model of communication, and integrating education work with health protection efforts and with preventive activities such as screening. The challenge of co-ordination within a primary care team is a pressing one. We believe that every primary care team should have a nominated co-ordinator for health promotion, who should liaise with a health education/ promotion officer concerned either specifically with primary care throughout a health board area or sub-area (or health district), or with the various settings and groups in a particular community patch. The role of the co-ordinator would build on the successes of the Oxford 'facilitator' model (Fullard *et al.* 1987), while taking into account the broad-based approach to health promotion espoused here.

6.5 Health promotion and a key setting—schools

There are several reasons why the school is a key setting for health promotion. First, in accordance with a 'prevention is better than cure' philosophy, it is better to encourage young people to adopt healthful lifestyles than to try to change unhealthful behaviour patterns in adulthood. Secondly, there is evidence (notably in relation to CHD) that the risk factors for disease in adulthood often originate early in life. Thirdly, schools provide a unique opportunity to augment other influences on health-related behaviour with properly planned programmes of health education, whereby inputs in relevant subject areas, such as biology, home economics, and physical education, are co-ordinated with one another, and may be complemented by a programme of personal, social, and health education.

Our discussions so far in this chapter have taken a deliberately fragmented look at health promotion in order to illustrate the model fully. In this example we seek to examine health promotion less artificially and more cohesively, starting with a look at health education as a whole in the school setting.

6.5.1 Health education in schools

Traditionally, health education in schools was concerned with 'hygiene and cleanliness', with minimizing the risks of infection. Partly as a result of the changing patterns of ill-health and largely due to recognition of the broader scope of health issues, the amount and breadth of health education in schools have increased greatly. Many of the changes can be linked to the ideas and models presented in earlier chapters.

Official recommendations have been made for a co-ordinated approach to health education in schools. Similar to our recommendations for primary care, the presence of a named co-ordinator in each school has been advocated.

Modern approaches to curriculum development in health education have emphasized the principle of the 'spiral curriculum', issues being dealt with in appropriate ways at appropriate ages. They have also taken a lifeskills approach, stressing concepts such as self-esteem, empowerment, and decision-making skills, rather than a purely information-based approach (Schools Council 1977*a*, *b*; 1982). This requires small-group teaching methods.

Schools offer an excellent opportunity for such labour-intensive efforts to educate for positive health simultaneously with attention to health hazards and available preventive services.

Much research has shown school-based health education to be capable of producing positive effects on beliefs, attitudes, and behaviour, both short- and long-term. It has, however, been repeatedly found that the outcomes predicted from formal evaluation are not necessary achieved in practice. One reason for this is the conflicting messages presented to young people in schools: attention to self-empowerment may be at odds with pupils' lack of control over their lives at school; teaching about the benefits of good nutrition may clash with practical cookery classes or the food served in the canteen; advocacy of the need for health protection measures may fall in the face of smoking in the staff-room. The point is that even 'modern' approaches to health education in schools, comprehensively planned, are not enough on their own. The school as a whole must become a health-promoting environment, in terms of ethos, policies, and provision.

6.5.2 The school as a health-promoting institution

Health education may be supplemented by the provision of appropriate preventive services, such as rubella immunization and dental measures, within the school. Moreover, health education may be reinforced by the provision of a positively healthful and safe environment in the school through regulatory action, affecting teachers as well as pupils. An important aspect of health protection in schools would be to ensure that exercise facilities are seen as available to all pupils rather than only to the sporting élite: this would be expected to enhance self-esteem as well as physical fitness.

6.5.3 Beyond the school

Another potential reason for a lack of success in schools' health promotion is that of 'culture clash' between the school and the home and elsewhere. This can occur when values promoted at school conflict with mores in families, peer groups, and so on. It follows, then, that schools' health promotion must be linked to efforts to influence the broader social environment. Once again health education/promotion officers have an important part to play.

6.6 Conclusions

1. The appearance of a new threat to health may warrant a specific, topic-based health education initiative aimed, for example, at securing health protection action. Where the new hazard is a product, the health education initiative may be best kept low-key in nature, to prevent the inadvertent stimulation of awareness of, and demand for, the harmful product.

2. The obtaining, through education, of local regulatory action may compensate for an absence of official control.

3. The model of health promotion presented in Chapter 4 may be used as a planning framework for action against a specific disease or risk factor. The model is, however, best used for the full exploration of health promotion opportunities in key community settings and with key groups, leading to the development of integrated programmes tailored to the needs of these settings and groups.

4. Primary health care and schools are vitally important settings for integrated programmes of health promotion. In both cases there is a pressing need to tap the potential more fully.

Acknowledgement

We are grateful to Mrs Diane Fenner, formerly Regional Health Promotion Officer, East Anglian Regional Health Authority, for her kind permission to present the campaign against snuff-dipping as a case study.

Part 2　Values

Introduction to Part 2

Some of our key concepts in Part 1 were modelled in terms of values—health in terms of well-being arising from the exercise of basic human qualities, and health education and promotion as processes which enhance that well-being. It is therefore helpful to think of the knowledge or technical base and the value or moral base of health promotion in terms of the analogy of a seamless garment. In discussing values we are simply turning the garment round and looking at the weaving from another angle.

We begin Part 2 with a discussion of the nature of attitudes and how they can be changed. Attitudes are perhaps the central concepts of the book because they are a focus for beliefs, feelings, and behaviour, and therefore express our values. Lasting changes to the health of a community must therefore come about through changes in attitudes, both personal and societal.

We consider in some detail what it is to value something, and what are the values which are essential to the flourishing of a society and an individual. These values we link via the idea of autonomy. But, since people are essentially social, autonomy is best expressed in the concept of citizenship. We repeat the point, which was stressed in Part 1, that autonomy is not something everyone in fact has—it is something to be achieved. To be a citizen, in the true sense, is to be *empowered*.

This conception does not fit easily with the traditional ideas of liberalism. In our view of health promotion, people should not see themselves as independent pursuers of their own interests; there is a communal good as well as individual goods—this is what is meant by calling people 'citizens'. Health promotion can be seen, from the perspective of Part 2, as an attempt to make this ideal of the citizen a reality. In particular, modifications of the liberal position arise in our conception of social justice.

Sometimes it is said that traditional medicine and health care are scientific and based on fact, whereas health promotion is moralistic; medicine deals with the 'is' and health promotion deals with the 'ought'. This view, which is generally intended as a criticism of health promotion, is confused. The truth is that *both* medicine *and* health promotion have a scientific basis, and *both* deal with prescriptions for improving the quality of life. The differences are between perspectives: the individual and the societal; the negative and the positive; the curative and the preventive; the reductivist and the holistic.

To say this is to say nothing necessarily disparaging of either; many of those in health care or health promotion can adopt either point of view as appropriate. Both points of view strive to be scientific, but neither is value-neutral. In this part of the book we try to express the scientifically based theory of health promotion in its value setting, which is nothing less than that of the good society—one which is conducive to the pursuit of 'a state of complete physical, mental, and social well-being'.

7 Attitudes, beliefs, and behaviour

Attitudes are central to health promotion since they tie together our feelings and beliefs. Also, as we shall see in Chapter 9, our values can be regarded as a subset of our attitudes. Feelings, beliefs, and values are all important determinants of our health-related behaviour. It is therefore of central importance to health promotion to consider what attitudes are and how they can be changed. The latter consideration is examined in Chapter 8. In this chapter we explore the concept of an attitude.

The relationship between attitudes and behaviour, and situational influences on this relationship, are of particular interest. Are attitudes predictive of behaviour? Will a change in an attitude necessarily result in a change in behaviour? And conversely, is attitude change a prerequisite for behavioural change? What factors affect these relationships?

It is important that these issues are examined in relation to health promotion, not because behavioural change is always the desired outcome but because we have to be clear about the consequences which can realistically be expected from programmes that effect a change in attitudes.

7.1 What is an attitude?

A number of definitions of an attitude exist, of which we shall examine two. Roediger *et al.* (1984; p. 587) define an attitude as 'a relatively stable tendency to respond consistently to particular people, objects, or situations'. This definition raises several points.

Firstly, attitudes are '*relatively stable*'; they are not fixed, and therefore, they change and can be changed. Secondly, the phrase '*tendency to respond consistently*' implies that a person's behavioural response in a situation provides an indication of their attitude towards it. By observing someone's behaviour it is possible to deduce their attitudes. However, the qualifier that it is a '*tendency*

to respond consistently' indicates that it is possible to behave incon-
sistently with one's attitudes. A person's behaviour does not necessarily represent those attitudes in a straightforward manner.

There are three reasons why this may be so. The first is that a
person's attitude may on some occasions not lead to the corresponding behaviour because a strong desire may lead to action inconsistent with the attitude. For example, a person may have a favourable
attitude towards losing weight, but be overcome by a strong desire to
eat rich food. This is the old-fashioned problem of 'weakness of
will'. Of course, if such desires consistently dominate the person's
behaviour we may come to doubt the existence of the favourable
attitude towards losing weight. But an occasional lapse is consistent
with the existence of the attitude, although lapses make inferences
from behaviour to attitudes uncertain.

The second reason for the uncertainty of inference from behaviour to attitude is that people have many attitudes, and these may on
occasion conflict. For example, a favourable attitude to losing
weight may be held at the same time as a favourable attitude to
courtesy, or to a specific hostess, and the result may be that a rich
meal is accepted, inconsistent with the favourable attitude to diet
but consistent with the favourable attitude to courtesy.

There is a third reason why a person's attitude, or intent to behave
in a particular way, may not result in the corresponding behaviour
being shown. The behaviour may not ensue if it conflicts with social,
cultural, or group norms; if it is discordant with the individual's
perceptions of what is acceptable behaviour.

These exceptions do not contradict the phrase 'a tendency to
respond consistently' but they alert us to situations where behaviour
may be inconsistent with attitudes.

Thirdly, the definition states that an attitude is a 'relatively stable
tendency to respond consistently *to particular people, objects or
situations*'. In other words, an attitude must be *towards* something.
This raises the question: 'Can an attitude be held towards anything?'. The answer is 'Yes', although it seems trivial to talk about
holding attitudes towards some things. The important point for our
purposes is that it is possible to hold an attitude towards another
attitude. For example, an elderly person may have an attitude of
fear or anxiety towards falling or being left alone, but at the same
time have an attitude of contempt towards the first attitude. Those
dealing with the elderly will be familiar with the problems such
conflicts of attitudes may bring with them. Conflicts of attitudes of

this kind can also be helpful, as we shall see later, in bringing about attitude change, for where a favourable attitude towards health exists it provides something on which health education can get a grip in order to weaken potentially unhealthful attitudes, such as favourable attitudes to rich food.

The definition given by Roediger *et al.* may be compared with the fuller definition of Ribeaux and Poppleton (1978): 'an attitude is a learned predisposition to think, feel and act in a particular way towards a given object or class of objects'. If we now examine that definition, several points are raised.

Firstly, an attitude is a '*learned predisposition*'. Now, it is true that learning is sometimes a conscious process involving understanding, but sometimes we learn without noticing that we are doing so. Similarly, an attitude may be changed as a result of consciously acquired knowledge and understanding, but this is not always the case. For example, a person's attitude towards pain killers may be changed by an advertisement for a new product which 'relieves pain faster'. He or she does not need to learn *why* the new product relieves pain faster in order to hold a favourable attitude towards, and be more likely to buy the new product. It seems, then, that attitudes are not necessarily *consciously* '*learned* predispositions'. Rather, they might sometimes be more accurately said to be 'acquired'.

Attitudes are acquired on the basis of some experience or evidence, either direct or indirect. For example, a favourable attitude towards the new pain killer might be acquired through direct experience that it does 'relieve pain faster'; or through indirect evidence of being told that it does so. What is clear is that attitudes are not fixed at birth, but rather are acquired in some way at some stage in life. In this sense, they are clearly distinct from instincts.

Ribeaux and Poppleton's definition also states that an attitude is a '*predisposition to think, feel and act in a particular way*'. There are three aspects, then, to an attitude—the cognitive, or belief aspect; the affective, or feeling aspect; and the conative, or behavioural aspect. So, as with the Roediger definition, an attitude is seen to be related to behaviour. In addition, however, cognitive and affective aspects are said to be present. We can regard the cognitive aspect as an active, conscious belief; the affective aspect as a nonrational, gut-reaction feeling; and the conative aspect as observed behaviour.

The two definitions examined here represent distinct viewpoints. Roediger's may be regarded as unidimensional. It focuses on only one component of an attitude, namely 'the tendency to respond'. No indication is given of different classes or types of response. Ribeaux and Poppleton's definition, on the other hand, is a three-component model of attitudes. Indeed, it goes beyond defining an attitude, and gives an indication of attitude structure. The three components appear separate but are not completely unrelated.

There are contradictory conclusions from the research that has been carried out to test which of these two models provides a more accurate description of attitudes (Chaiken and Stangor 1987). As we shall see later, the unidimensional model is that most frequently adopted, for simplicity in measurement, in attempts to measure attitudes. For other purposes within the field of health promotion, the three-component model seems to be the more useful. We shall now examine the three components in more detail, with respect to health-related attitudes.

7.2 The three aspects of attitudes

The *cognitive component* concerns the individual's belief about the object or attitude. This belief may not be a true or accurate representation of the facts—it may be biased or incomplete. But it represents the individual's own direct or indirect intellectual evaluation of the object, based on facts collected or acquired.

As we have said, however, beliefs are not always based on the weight of objective evidence; they can also be based on inaccurate personal estimations. From the point of view of health promotion this latter aspect is the more important and the more problematic (Tones 1981). While it has been found to be a relatively straightforward task to change people's *general* beliefs about health-related behaviour, their beliefs about *their own* susceptibility to disease or the effectiveness of interventions are less easily changed. For example, most people have been convinced by frequent presentations of the evidence that there are impressive correlations between smoking and lung cancer, but some people continue to believe that, in their particular case, smoking will not cause lung cancer on the grounds that, say, a grandfather or neighbour smoked all his life and lived until he was ninety.

Inaccurate personal estimations of evidence (which are expressions of the cognitive component of an attitude) are also influenced by, and themselves influence, the *affective component* of an attitude—feelings, likes and dislikes, and emotions. The affective component is also important for health promotion. For example, a child may believe that the eating of sweets or sugary foods can damage the teeth and therefore that it is a bad thing to do. Nevertheless, the child may like sweets, experience enjoyment when eating them, and therefore eat them!

A person's feelings are also influenced by his or her values. A great deal more will be said about values in Chapter 9 so it is sufficient here to state that our values are about how things *ought* to be, and serve as the standards by which we assess the way things are. The affective component of an attitude, then, is concerned not with an intellectual evaluation of the situation but with feelings about it, and such feelings can be influenced by the value system which we hold.

The *conative component* is the behavioural component of an attitude. The term 'behaviour' takes in a wide range of phenomena, verbal and non-verbal, including consciously effected actions and even physiological reactions. These events also take place within a range of environmental situations which will themselves influence behaviour. There is difficulty, then, in assuming that what a person says or does is an accurate reflection of his or her attitude. A distinction has been drawn, for example, between attitudes and opinions (e.g. Wheldall 1975). An opinion is a publicly stated expression of an attitude, but the true attitude held may only be expressed in situations where there is trust and privacy. Thus, opinion polls are exactly that, and cannot be taken as an accurate and valid indication of people's true attitudes because publicly observable behaviour does not necessarily represent the attitude of interest.

The most frequently cited example of this is the experiment carried out by La Piere (1934). In the early 1930s, a time of widespread anti-Asian prejudice, La Piere travelled throughout the USA with a Chinese couple. They were refused service in only one of over 200 establishments. Six months later, La Piere wrote to all these establishments asking if they would accept Chinese guests. Of those who responded, 92 per cent said that they would not. These statements clearly contradict the behaviour that was displayed. This lack of correlation is not supported by all studies examining the attitude—behaviour relationship, however (Ajzen and Fishbein 1977). One explanation may be the need to consider the different dimensions within the concepts of attitudes and behaviour (see below).

The question next arises as to whether all three components of an attitude (the cognitive, affective, and conative) have to be present, and if so whether they all need to coincide. Consider the example of someone who knows that millions of people are starving in the Third World and that this starvation could be lessened by a reduction in food consumption, and in particular the consumption of meat, in developed countries. That person might also feel that this situation is morally wrong and can be changed, but might still continue to eat large, meat-based meals. In this case, the person could be said to hold an attitude sympathetic to the starving people in the Third World on the basis of the cognitive and affective aspects. His or her behaviour, however, is unchanged by the possession of this attitude, so the conative aspect of the attitude is lacking. Many other exam-· ples could illustrate the same point: the possession of an attitude does not necessitate that the person thinks, feels, and acts in a particular way. Not all three aspects are necessarily present.

The argument so far has described attitudes as having three components, which we have called the cognitive, affective, and conative aspects. This, however, is only one way of examining the structure of attitudes and we shall now present another analysis which deals with the *dimensions* of attitudes.

We have already implied, firstly, that attitudes have *direction*, that they are positive, negative, or neutral. We can now develop this characterization by adding further dimensions, beginning with extremeness and strength. *Extremeness* refers to the extent of direction, to how positive or negative the attitude is. *Strength* can be regarded as an indication of the stability of an attitude, of its resistance to change. It is a product of extremeness together with the length of time for which the attitude has been held, and like extremeness it is also affected by the individual's own personality, the attitudes of the reference groups to which the subject belongs, and the degree of integration of this attitude with his or her other attitudes. A fourth dimension of attitude, the degree to which it is related to and integrated with other attitudes, is known as the *isolation* of the attitude. The less isolated an attitude, the more resistant it is to change.

A fifth relevant dimension is the *cognitive content*. People may hold the same attitude but for different reasons. For example, a positive attitude towards a new pain killer will have a shallow cognitive depth (and be relatively unstable) if it has arisen solely as a result of seeing the television advert for it. It will have greater cognitive depth (and be relatively stable) if it has arisen from a knowledge of the biochemical innovation from which the pain killer has resulted. Finally, attitudes have a sixth dimension of *differentiation* or sophistication. This is a measurement of how clear or structured the attitude is.

Each of these six dimensions—direction, extremeness, strength, isolation, cognition, and differentiation—affects the stability of an attitude; and the complexity of their interrelationship provides an indication of the problems to be faced when trying to effect change in attitudes.

A different characterization of the dimensions of attitudes and behaviour was presented by Ajzen and Fishbein (1977). They identified four specific elements:

1. The *action* element (i.e. *what* behaviour is to be performed).
2. The *target* element (i.e. *at what target* the behaviour is to be directed).
3. The *context* element (i.e. *in what context* the behaviour is to be performed).
4. The *time* element (i.e. *when* the behaviour is to be performed).

They argued that observations of a lack of correlation between attitudes and behaviour are sometimes due to the fact that measurements made of the two often do not correspond in their degree of specificity in relation to the four identified elements.

Having examined the different components and dimensions of attitudes, and become aware of the complexity of the concept, let us now examine the practical issues involved in first identifying and then measuring people's attitudes.

7.3 Methods of identifying attitudes

Given that the cognitive, affective, and conative aspects need not coincide, and indeed do not all need to be present, how can we identify the attitudes held by a person? Also, given the several dimensions of an attitude, can we be sure of what it is that we are measuring? It may be assumed that the most strongly held attitudes are those in which thinking, believing, and acting are all present and coincident. These attitudes will be the easiest to identify and the most difficult to change. In less strongly held attitudes there may be some dissonance between the components. There seem to be two ways of determining which attitudes are held:

1. By asking people *directly* what is their attitude towards the situation of interest.

2. By observation of people's behaviour—the way they respond to particular people, objects, or situations—and thereby *indirectly* identifying their attitude.

The first method—asking directly what attitude is held—is problematical in that the response received will reflect situational factors as well as the subject's true feelings. For example, when asked to state their attitude towards something, people often offer the response which they think is the 'correct' one, or which they think the interviewer 'wants to hear'. Nevertheless, it is possible to formulate the questions in such a way that this problem is minimized.

The second method—observation of behaviour—is not without its own difficulties since it assumes that behaviour is a true reflection of the attitudes held by a person. We have already illustrated that this is not necessarily the case—the behavioural component of an attitude is not always present, and, even when it is, it is not necessarily concordant with the other components of the attitude. In some situations, however, behaviour is reasonably regarded as a true reflection of a person's attitude. For example, while patients may be reluctant to express disapproval during a consultation about new procedures introduced by their GP in the health centre, if they uncharacteristically fail to reattend the surgery, or if they change their doctor, we might reasonably assume that they hold a negative attitude towards the new procedures. Similarly, while many doctors will express disapproval and contempt for drug companies' promotions of their products via lavish free lunches, their willingness to attend such events can be taken as an indication of their true feelings. Moreover, often it does not really matter what people say they would do in a situation; it is what they actually *do* do that affects policies. Thus, even if opinion polls indicate that a large proportion of the community want to use a particular sports facility, if attendance figures are too low to indicate a demand, then the facility will no longer receive economic backing. Clearly, then, although we must be wary about extrapolating from behaviour to attitudes, it may often be valid for us to do so.

In some situations, of course, it is not possible to determine attitudes by observing behaviour. We may want to *predict* how people will behave under a new condition (such as the provision of a totally non-smoking bar) or we may want to examine attitudes to some *hypothetical* situation (a completely private health care system, for example). In cases such as these the first method—direct inquiry—is the only possible one.

7.4 Measuring attitudes

We have argued that attitudes have several dimensions. If we are to be able to measure them we therefore need a means of measurement that is sufficiently complex not only to identify which attitudes are held but also to determine their strength and stability. We have discussed the problems of identifying attitudes indirectly by observing behaviour, so here we concentrate on direct methods of measurement. Such measures are called *attitude scales*. They provide a means of quantifying variables and usually involve a choice from a range of numerical values. The evaluation process is 'a process where a set of elements is divided into three parts (trichotomized): "positive", "neutral or indifferent", and "negative" elements' (Galtung 1967; p. 90). In practice the gradation seldom stops at this, as there are shades of positive and negative. Only the neutral category is usually held to be indivisible. Several principles should be followed in the creation of attitude scales.

Firstly, there should be as many positive as negative symbols. Secondly, they should be symmetrically distributed relative to the neutral point—otherwise the set of values is biased. Thirdly, it is usually understood that the symbols form at least an ordinal scale. (An ordinal scale is composed of qualitative categories, such as social class, which have a distinct order but no inherent numerical distance between their values.)

The two principal methods involved in scale construction were developed by Likert (1932) and Thurstone (1928). Both of these methods are based on the assumption that attitudes can be measured by the opinions or beliefs of people about the objects of interest.

The Likert scale is a five-point scale used to evaluate statements. It is balanced around the neutral point, having the same number of positive and negative symbols. The respondent evaluates a series of statements which express positive or negative beliefs or feelings about the object in question, by indicating his or her degree of agreement on the scale. An attitude score is computed by summing the respondent's answers to different items. An example of a Likert scale item is as follows.

(*Score scale*)	+ 2	Strongly agree
	+ 1	Moderately agree
	1	Neither agree nor disagree
	– 1	Moderately disagree
	– 2	Strongly disagree

Thurstone's equal appearing interval scale (the 'Thurstone scale') is more complex. It is based on an 11-point rating scale indicating the amount of favourableness (or unfavourableness) towards the attitude object. The symbols on this scale originally were the letters A to K. In principle this was an interval scale (it being assumed that the difference between any two consecutive points was equal to that between any two others). The items to be rated in the final scale are selected from the ratings of a large pool of items by many judges. The final scale is composed of items covering the whole attitude continuum, with high inter-judge correlation and which different-iate between those judges with different attitudes.

A Thurstone scale is expensive and time-consuming to construct, and is rarely used now. Moreover, the interval nature of the scale is highly dubious. Because of this difficulty, and the problem of find-ing words corresponding to five levels of agreement and disagree-ment, scales are often represented graphically as a ladder or a thermometer, for example, and the respondent indicates the 'warmth' of his or her feelings towards the object. These graphical scales introduce the interval structure which is absent when the symbols are words.

One problem with the 'pure' Thurstone and Likert scales is that a new scale of items has to be constructed for each new attitude object. The *semantic differential technique* (Osgood *et al.* 1957) is a scale with which it is possible to measure different attitudes. It consists of a series of bipolar ratings which have been found to be appropriate for describing a person's attitude to the object in ques-tion. The respondent's attitude is calculated from the total of the scores (which usually vary from + 3 to – 3) from each rating scale. An example of ratings used in semantic differential scales is as follows.

Good	+ 3	+ 2	+ 1	0	– 1	– 2	– 3	Bad
Pleasant	+ 3	+ 2	+ 1	0	– 1	– 2	– 3	Unpleasant
Clean	+ 3	+ 2	+ 1	0	– 1	– 2	– 3	Dirty

The fact that we can measure attitudes by these methods is impor-tant when we consider strategies for changing peoples attitudes towards health and health services. Because of the interrelationship between attitudes and beliefs and behaviour, influencing attitudes is a central aim of health promotion. The measurement of attitudes before and then after intervention provides an indication of the effectiveness of strategies for attitude change. Several such strategies exist (see Chapter 8) but an understanding of their effects is based on the psychological theories of attitude change. It is, therefore, to these theories that we shall now turn.

7.5 Theories of attitude change

The most useful theories for explaining attitude change are *cognitive consistency theories* based on Heider's theory of consistency (Heider 1944). The argument is that people strive to have their own 'cognitions' (beliefs, attitudes, and perceptions) organized in a tension-free manner. Tension arises when cognitions are contradictory, resulting in the person being motivated to bring them into a tension-free state. We shall examine two theories of cognitive consistency: balance theory and cognitive dissonance theory.

According to Heider's *balance theory* (Heider 1958), tension alone is not sufficient to generate attitude change—the individual must become *aware* of the imbalance. When imbalance is discovered there are three possible types of outcome:

1. The direction of one or more of the cognitions can be changed.

2. One or more of the elements can be redefined.

3. The individual can cease to think about the matter and thus restore cognitive consistency.

Imagine, for example, the position of the schoolboy who discovers that his role models smoke cigarettes but who himself believes that this is an unhealthy, dirty habit. He is in a state of tension because people for whom he has great admiration and respect (and towards whom he has strong positive attitudes) are displaying a pattern of behaviour which he regards as dangerous and unpleasant (towards which he has strong negative attitudes). To reduce this state of tension he may, in the first instance, decide that cigarette smoking is not dangerous and dirty after all, and thus change the direction of his attitude towards smoking. In the second instance he might redefine the behaviour of his role models by deciding that what they are doing is not in fact smoking cigarettes in a dangerous and dirty way—perhaps they are not inhaling the smoke, or are only smoking small numbers of cigarettes. His third option is to ignore the inconsistency. Balance theory does not predict which of these outcomes will occur.

Cognitive dissonance theory was proposed by Festinger (1957) and differs from balance theory in that it includes actions. People's attitudes are taken to determine their behaviour. When attitudes conflict, or conflict with behaviour, cognitive dissonance results in a change of attitudes or behaviour such that they come back into harmony. Cognitive dissonance theory helps us to predict what will happen when people are forced to do or say something contrary to their private belief. For illustration we can refer to an experiment by Festinger and Carlsmith (1959), as follows.

Two groups carried out boring, pointless tasks. Group A were paid $1 and told to inform the next subject that the tasks had been fun and interesting. Group B were paid $20 to do the same thing. When asked afterwards for their real opinion of the interest of the task, it was rated higher by the $1 group than by the $20 group. According to cognitive dissonance theory, Group B could justify lying to their successors because they were adequately rewarded for doing so. For Group A, on the other hand, the sum of money involved was so small that it did not justify lying. They could not explain their lying behaviour by reference to the external factor of a reward. Consequently, they experienced dissonance as a result of lying about the boring tasks. The dissonance was resolved by redefining the tasks as interesting.

Cognitive dissonance theory also enables us to make predictions about the way in which people expose themselves to information. It predicts that people seek information in such a way as to maintain cognitive consonance, or avoid cognitive dissonance. They are motivated to expose themselves to attitude-consonant information (that which is concordant with their existing attitudes) and to avoid attitude-dissonant information. This *selective exposure hypothesis* has been supported by research findings (e.g. Frey 1986). This research also identified the conditions under which people act contrary to the selective exposure hypothesis, and expose themselves to dissonant information. They will do so either (1) when their cognitions are relatively weak, and it seems better to change them to be consonant with the new information; or (2) when their cognitive system is strong and they can argue against new information and accommodate it in balance with existing attitudes. These research findings have important implications for the strategies for attitude change which are discussed in the following chapter.

7.6 Conclusions

1. Attitudes are central to our understanding of people's behaviour. Attitudes are affected by beliefs and values and may be reflected in feelings and behaviour.
2. Attitudes are relatively stable entities, but are not fixed. They change and can be changed.
3. Attitudes are acquired through personal experiences, the main influences being the immediate primary groups such as family and friends, although secondary influences such as the school, and peer or reference groups are also extremely important to the formation of attitudes. (The tertiary influences of the media will be considered in the next chapter.)
4. Attitudes have several functions. They enable us to filter and order our experiences, and can also justify or support our behaviour, as in the case of attitudes of disbelief held by smokers. Moreover, we can attract attention by expressing certain attitudes rather than others. If these attitudes are approved by others, this results in reinforcement and consequently these attitudes will increase in strength.
5. Identification of attitudes held can be carried out either by direct questioning or by behaviour observation. Each method has disadvantages, but care with methodology can increase the reliability of results.
6. Measurement of attitudes is possible, but complex scales are needed because of the several dimensions of attitudes.
7. Psychological theories of attitude change bring out the complex nature of these concepts. Attitudes can be changed by a challenge to the knowledge or value base, or by altering people's behaviour. Both of these approaches have been employed in health promotion initiatives.

8 Strategies for changing attitudes

Attitudes can be changed in two main ways. Firstly, they can be changed by the provision of information which is inconsistent with current beliefs. For example, information may be presented by books, newspapers, magazines, and leaflets; or by the spoken word through tapes or the radio; or in a visual manner by film, TV, or lecture. All these vehicles may provide information which conflicts with a person's beliefs. Secondly, attitudes can be changed by making people behave in a manner which is inconsistent with their current beliefs. This can be done either by direct exposure to the attitude object, for example by role-play or directed observation; or by changing the rewards and costs of different courses of behaviour, by legislation for example. In this chapter we shall examine all these methods, and in later chapters take account of the impact of values on these strategies.

8.1 Providing information

Attitudes, we have said, can be changed by the provision of information which is inconsistent with a person's current beliefs. The mere repeated exposure of an individual to a stimulus has been shown to be sufficient to enhance his or her attitude towards it (Zajonc 1968). Nevertheless, people are bombarded daily with a mass of information and only a small proportion of it ever 'sticks'. The information may be ignored; it may be acknowledged, but may not stick; it may stick for a short time and then be forgotten; or, indeed, it may stick and remain but be disbelieved or redefined. The aim, then, is to present information in a way that will be attractive and have immediate appeal to people, and cause it to be accepted and retained.

People's attitudes are affected by factors other than the credibility of the information and the position being put across. For example, the greater people's liking for the communicator the more likely it is they will be open to the arguments. Similarly, the message that is presented and the manner in which it is communicated are also integral to the effectiveness of attempts to change attitudes.

There are several factors involved in the provision of information for attitude change. They can be summed up by the phrase, 'who says what to whom and in what way'. In this phrase 'who' is the communicator, 'what' is the communication or message, 'whom' is the audience, and the 'way' is the medium of communication. We shall look at these factors in turn.

8.1.1 The communicator

Liking and similarity—The greater people's liking for the communicator, the more likely they are to be open to his or her arguments. The most powerful traits that cause liking seem to be loyalty, honesty, sincerity, competence, and physical attractiveness. There is also evidence that people like others who have opinions similar to their own; and who are dressed and groomed in a similar way to themselves. In short, a message is more likely to be accepted if it is delivered by someone who has similarities with the audience, and who is honest and sincere about the message he or she is putting across.

Intentions—Walster and Festinger (1962) have found that a message is more effective if it is overheard rather than directed towards the listener. People become suspicious if they think that the communicator is trying to persuade them of something. The 'soft sell' was devised to avoid this effect: but the problem is that the sell may become too soft and fail to make any impact! However, the implication is that a message about the dangers of transmission of human immunodeficiency virus (HIV) via infected needles, for example, might be more effective at changing attitudes among drug users if it is 'overheard' rather than aimed directly at them. In addition, if the intentions of the communicator are perceived as honest he or she is more likely to produce attitude change.

Prestige—In general, the greater the prestige possessed by the communicator the greater the change in attitudes he or she is likely to produce. Aronson *et al.* (1963) found that an enthusiastic review of a piece of modern poetry had more effect in changing subjects' attitudes if it was said to be by T.S. Eliot than by an unknown female student. People are not foolish enough to believe information just because it is told to them. They need to have some basis for judging its credibility.

Reference groups—Members of reference groups can be effective in influencing people's attitudes in two ways: by changing their opinions to make them agree with the rest of the group, and by supporting a member's opinion so he or she can resist persuasion from outside the group.

The use of group members, or opinion leaders within a community, as a source of information can therefore be an effective strategy for changing attitudes. However, the other role of group members, that of 'insulating' current attitudes and resisting change, should not be forgotten.

8.1.2 The communication

The information must be useful and relevant to the recipients— Information is much more likely to be attended to and retained if it has relevance for the person at that moment. Few of us store up information in the hope that it will come in useful some day. To use advertising terms, the message has to be slanted to the consumer's needs.

Positive information is preferred—There is evidence that people attend more to 'good' news than bad, especially when they are forming an opinion or when their commitment to an opinion is low. Think of how health educators have shifted from the threatening 'If you smoke you die' approach, to the more positive one of 'You can taste your food' or 'You can run for a bus'.

The message should be put in a simple way—Information often fails to get across because the message is too complicated. Professionals have a tendency to set their standards too high, in a desire to ensure that they pass critical comment from their fellow professional 'experts' in the field. This they may do: but the 'ignorant' public remain confused.

Novelty of the information—If the recipients believe that they are about to hear something new, they are more likely to change their attitude towards the subject after hearing the message. This principle also extends to the use of 'alternative' methods, such as art, drama, and humour, for transmitting the information.

Several other factors about the communication have been found to have a marginal effect. For example, by *stating a conclusion* the communicator can make sure that the target audience knows what has been said. On the other hand, by not stating one, the communicator is less likely to give the impression of trying to convince the audience of his or her point of view (see above). Other points to be considered are the relative advantages of *one-sided* versus *two-sided information*, and the *order of presentation* where both sides of the argument are being presented. Again, the effect seems to vary with the audience. The less informed and intelligent the audience, the more likely that one-sided communication will be effective. In most situations, though, two-sided communication is more effective—possibly because communicators are likely to seem better informed, less biased, and less as though they are trying to influence the audience.

8.1.3 The audience

Commitment—In general terms, the more important the issue is to the audience, the more they will be affected by the quality of the argument presented rather than by 'secondary' factors such as aspects of the communicator, the situation, and so on. On the other hand, secondary factors are more influential when the issue is less important to the listeners, and they are therefore less motivated to attend.

If a person has voluntarily become committed to a course of action, any communication denying the rightness of that action is likely to be rejected. One variable affecting the degree of commitment is whether the subject had free choice in taking the given course of action. Freedman and Steinbruner (1964) found that subjects who had been made to feel that they had made up their minds freely on a given subject were more resistant to changing their opinions than were those who were made to feel they had little choice in their decisions. (This finding is very much in line with cognitive dissonance theory.)

Personality factors—Hovland and Janis (1959) have shown that subjects who are persuasible under one set of conditions tend also to be so under others. It is not clear which personality factors are responsible for this tendency although it has been found fairly consistently that subjects low in self-esteem are more persuasible. Also, women have been found to be more open to persuasion than men. Intelligence is another factor which is related to persuasibility in certain circumstances. However, the relationship is not a direct one, as is illustrated by the finding that intelligent people become more persuasible if a conclusion is not stated (see above).

Avoid the use of arguments that are too extreme for the audience—People judge new information in terms of how they already feel about a topic. Any argument that differs too much from their current beliefs on a topic will be rejected. This means that a communicator should not decide on the arguments to use before finding out the attitudes presently held by an audience. Moreover, the communicator should not expect a major change from these presently held attitudes, except by gradual progress over time.

In addition to these general points, there are several other 'receiver factors' which will affect the effectiveness of attempts to change attitudes. For example, the likelihood of receivers' accepting the new information will be increased or decreased by their own perception of the amount of pressure acting on them towards conformity both to group, or cultural, norms and also their own personality type. Other influential 'receiver factors' include the amount of motivation receivers have to change their attitudes and to attend to the message; their memory and comprehension of the message; and the consequences of the attitude change for them in terms of reward or punishment. Whilst most of these factors are outwith the communicator's control, some of them may be alterable in his or her favour.

8.1.4 The small group

The medium used to convey information can be crucial to the success of attempts at changing attitudes. The superiority of audio-visual modalities over the written or spoken word is well attested in education technology. Although there have been fewer studies in the area of attitude change, there is sufficient evidence to suggest that film or video can be an effective way of informing the public.

The audio-visual medium has several clear advantages over the written word and also over audio-recordings. However, written words and recorded sound have their benefits as well, and should certainly not be discarded as media for providing information.

The written word—Information provided in books, magazines, leaflets, and so on is relatively inaccessible to those who either cannot read or are unlikely to apply themselves to comprehending and assimilating written information. It certainly needs to be presented in an attractive, interesting manner to encourage people to read. There are several ways of doing this. Zimmerman (1985), for example, proposes the use of humour as an effective way of presenting messages. Humour often allows people to see the problem in a different perspective—and certainly can create a mood in which other positive emotions, such as enthusiasm and hope, can emerge.

The written word provides a medium for presenting a case in its entirety, without interruption. It does now allow for discussion or questioning, but its big advantages are its relative permanency and its visibility.

Audio recordings—Audio recordings have limitations as means of providing information for attitude change. They suffer from many of the same disadvantages as the written word without its advantages. For example, they provide no room for discussion and require a high level of concentration for comprehension of the message being transmitted.

We have noted above that people are more receptive to information presented by someone similar to themselves. The voice is one indicator of similarity, and in this sense audio-recordings could have an advantage over the written word if the communicator is matched with the target audience.

Audio-visual methods—Audio-visual methods are most effective if they incorporate some of the ingredients already identified: presentation by a credible, prestigious presenter—giving positive information honestly, and in a simple and relevant form. Several studies have elicited changes in viewers' attitudes following a visual presentation. The differences were not as great as those found with a face-to-face meeting, but video proved decidedly superior to audio-recordings of the same events.

In the area of changing attitudes towards disability, film has proved unsuccessful when it has taken the form of a factual, educational-type production presented by a non-disabled person. In the same way, a film of handicapped children in wheelchairs participating in physical education with non-handicapped children, narrated by an adult, made little impression on 10 year-olds. The investigator (Forader 1970) concluded that 'film alone does not appear to be sufficient to handle all the questions that a non-handicapped child might have about a handicapped peer and its effect does not appear to be permanent'. This criticism, of course, may be as much of the *content* of the film as of the film as a medium. But we can accept the recommendation that film be used in conjunction with other experiences such as listening to handicapped speakers and participating in discussion sessions.

Clearly, the different media for providing information may be combined, with the result that limitations can be overcome and messages reinforced in different ways. Moreover, these media can be combined with *face-to-face contact*. This will be discussed further below, but it is important to emphasize here that the success of such contact, whether of an informal kind or in a more formal lecture setting, depends on the inclusion of the 'ingredients for success' outlined above. Where communicators have direct experience of the information they are providing, they are very powerful sources for attitude change. For example, disabled persons can contradict stereotypes of disability by their own personality; and AIDS sufferers also can negate stereotypes and prejudices by explaining their own experiences.

Direct face-to-face contact also provides the opportunity for discussion. Discussions should, however, be used cautiously, and it must be ensured that they are based on information rather than biased opinions or emotions.

This look at the various media for providing information has so far been centred upon the individual or small group situation. When we talk of changing social attitudes we are talking about changing the attitudes of individuals (for only individuals can hold attitudes) and so these 'tailor-made' methods are relevant. However, they have limitations in their labour-intensity for reaching large numbers of people. For this purpose we often turn to the mass media.

8.1.5 The mass media

'The temptation to look to the mass media to solve problems which affect the mass of people may be overwhelming but careful evaluation and costing is needed' (Howitt 1982; p. 168).

The mass media have clear advantages when it comes to providing information in that they reach vast numbers of people, and perhaps more importantly, they reach the groups in society who are less likely to have interpersonal contact with the 'experts'. For example, in health education it is particularly important to reach those who do not have direct contact with the health professions. Medrich (1979) found that the households with constantly tuned-in television sets had lower educational standards and income. Single parent households were well represented. That is, 'those with fewer material and cultural resources and those who also often live with less privacy in crowded homes' had peak exposure. And, of course, old, sick, infirm, or housebound people may be highly dependent on the media as a source of entertainment and information.

The mass media, however, are a two-edged weapon. For example, they may be an advocate of sickness as well as of health. There are several ways in which the media could promote ill-health:

— by advertising products which affect health: this advertising can take the form of either straightforward advertisements (e.g. alcohol, sugary foods, cigars, etc.), or the more subtle advertising of tobacco sponsorship of sport and the arts, or the use of public-house locations in 'soap operas';

— by neglecting to publicize information which demonstrates health risks attached to certain products;

— by decrying warnings of danger;

— by inadvertently encouraging the use of dangerous products by actively supporting substances which although less dangerous are similar.

It is therefore apparent that a close eye must be kept on the messages transmitted by the media.

Moreover, even when the mass media are explicitly attempting to change attitudes to health favourably, they are not always successful. For example, Maccoby and Farquhar (1975) evaluated a semi-experimental method designed to help people in Stanford (USA) change their coronary-producing behaviour (largely smoking and eating fatty acids). Three communities were selected which were as similar in size and other features as was practicable. The communities were surveyed to obtain baseline data on diet, exercise, and smoking. Subsequently, in community A there was no abnormal intervention; in community B there was an eight-month media campaign utilizing television, radio, newspapers, billboards, and a number of printed items; and in community C this media campaign was supplemented with intensive treatment of the individuals at risk. Results showed that the mass media alone did not improve 'health attitudes and behaviours' as much as the media and intensive treatment combined. However, the differential between the groups almost disappeared after two years.

This study indicated that media campaigns can have an effect, but that the effect is enhanced, at least for a time, if the campaign is supplemented by within-community interventions. Further studies have indicated in some instances that mass media efforts can be quite successful even in the absence of supplementary instruction. Certain kinds of behaviour (such as dietary changes) can be learned through exposure to mass media while others require a considerable amount of skills training (e.g. cigarette smoking cessation). Learning how to modify complex habitual behaviour, such as smoking, can be difficult, and the acquisition of such skills is enhanced by feedback and encouragement. These cannot be provided by the mass media.

Sutton and Hallett (1987), with their evaluation of the BBC TV series *So You Want to Stop Smoking*, also illustrated the lack of success of a media campaign in the area of smoking cessation. There was no clear evidence that the BBC series was more effective in encouraging smokers to try to stop and helping them succeed than a control film. On the other hand, Engleman's (1987) recent review of the impact of mass media anti-smoking publicity states that 'the most reasonable conclusion that can be drawn on the basis of the research reviewed . . . is that mass media anti-smoking publicity has both a significant and long-term impact on smoking.' We could perhaps conclude that, whereas within each particular social group exposed to the programmes the number who change their attitudes or behaviour is very small, the overall number who do is still high.

More conclusive is the research showing that the media and the community may interact to deal effectively with social issues. An example of this concerns contraception and family planning. Verbrugge (1978) described the results of a study begun in the late 1960s of the West Malaysian population policy. The main aim was to encourage the use of the contraceptive pill. Fewer than 10 per cent of women were using any form of contraception prior to the programme, so its importance was obvious. The study looked at what encouraged women to seek contraception early in the campaign. Primarily they were encouraged by personal sources. Husbands were the most important, followed by clinic nurses and friends, then neighbours and relatives. Only 7 per cent of the women claimed to have been *primarily influenced* by the mass media, but most had heard about family planning on the radio and about two-fifths had read something in the newspapers. Diversity in communication sources seemed to be a key feature in early acceptance of family planning, with the mass media increasing the ability of those accepting to pass on the message to other women 'eligible' for contraception.

Maccoby and Alexander (1980) also favour a diversity in communication sources, with mass media programmes integrated with interpersonal intervention. Their choice of the 'best' strategy for optimum efficiency of community-based attitude and behaviour change programmes is a plan which 'blends a minimal but focused amount of face-to-face instruction with an extensive media campaign that is strong enough to create the desired outcomes, in part, by itself' (p. 369).

The conclusion suggested by this discussion of the media is that while mass communication may be very useful, its effectiveness is greatly enhanced if it is combined with other methods of communication.

Some final points to be made about the provision of information for attitude change concern the *situational* or *background* factors to the communication. Even if all the ingredients described above for achieving a change in attitudes are followed, the attempt will not be successful if the situation is not conducive to change. Factors to be considered include:

Distraction—Distraction may prevent the message ever reaching the 'target'. On the other hand, in a lesser amount it may serve to facilitate the communication by distracting defences against persuasion.

Reinforcement—A communication is more likely to persuade the receiver if it is reinforced. For example, many business deals are said to be clinched over a good meal.

Fear arousal—A moderate amount of fear may enhance the persuasive effect of a communication. Extreme fear, however, may bring into action other factors such as the mechanism of denial; or it may disrupt someone so much that he or she is unable to act coherently.

To sum up, it seems clear that we can effectively change attitudes by the provision of information. There are many media available for the transmission of information and their relative effectiveness will depend on the situation and type of message being communicated. Research has clearly identified several 'ingredients for success' in the provision of information to change attitudes. Those hoping to effect a successful attitude change will greatly increase their chances by noting them.

8.2 Changing behaviour

The second strategy for changing social attitudes—by making people behave in a manner which is inconsistent with their current beliefs (counter-attitudinal behaviour)—is less widely applicable and has been less thoroughly researched than the provision of information. There are many situations in which it is clearly impossible, inappropriate, or unethical to change behaviour for the purpose of changing attitudes. For example, one cannot make people directly experience a nuclear winter in order to change their attitudes towards nuclear weaponry; nor can the colour of people's skins be changed to make them experience the racist reactions of people in society. There are only limited areas in which people's behaviour can be changed to enable them to experience directly and personally the relevant situation. However, in many cases it is possible to adapt people's behaviour so that they experience the situation through directed observation, or through role-play. We shall examine the use of these strategies in the field of changing attitudes towards disabled people.

8.2.1 Changing attitudes through contact with people

For the most of the public, their impressions of disabled people are not based on firsthand experiences. An obvious approach to community education, then, is to arrange for the public to meet disabled people. The theory is that they will then realize that their prejudices and stereotyped impressions are mistaken and their attitudes will change. This approach is, however, a high-risk one—some contacts between disabled people and the community have worsened rather than improved the public's perception.

The contact will be most successful if it gives disabled and non-disabled people the chance to talk to one another, share information and learn more about each other. But merely bringing people together is insufficient. It is important to plan what they will do. Ideally the disabled and non-disabled groups should participate in a common activity during which each can contribute to the overall outcome. The activities should be chosen with care. They must not exceed the capabilities of the disabled people who should be competent in the chosen tasks. Moreover, contexts in which disabled people have to depend on help from non-disabled partners should be avoided.

It should, as far as possible, be a meeting of equals, by selecting the disabled people to match the characteristics of the non-disabled group. This means, at the very least, matching children with children and adults with adults. Mixing adults and children has been less successful. Moreover, people's negative stereotypes of disability can be counteracted by presenting opportunities for disabled people to demonstrate what they can do rather than dwelling on their limitations. In this respect, it is perfectly legitimate to focus on the 'exceptional' rather than the stereotypical handicapped person. Otherwise the danger is that the public's tendency to underestimate is reinforced.

Studies have supported many of these common-sense recommendations. McConkey *et al.* (1983), for example, reported on their use in the field of changing young people's perceptions of those who are mentally handicapped. In this study, 15-and 16-year-old school students met young mentally handicapped adults; the two groups successfully participated in table-top games, such as draughts and card games; and the students watched a video of mentally handicapped workers tackling a complex weaving job. Each of these components of the contact was successful in inducing a positive change in attitudes. Four months later the students completed questionnaires to see if these effects were maintained. By and large they were, although there was some falling off. This implies that regular meetings may be necessary to maintain attitude change.

A final point should be made concerning contact with disabled persons, and it is applicable to other situations as well. Some people openly state that the presence of a disabled person is unnerving for them; and it is likely that most people feel some discomfort. It is vital, therefore, to put people at their ease. Prior to the contact it is useful to provide guidance on how to interact. This information will be more effective if it comes from a disabled person or other credible source. There must be an enjoyable atmosphere at the meeting, and pleasant comfortable surroundings. Also, people's tendency to stare at the unfamiliar creates extra tension in the context of meeting disabled people. Some have argued that people need the opportunity to engage in 'sanctioned staring'—looking at photographs or watching videos of disabled people.

8.2.2 Changing attitudes through experiential learning

One of the most promising techniques in experiential learning is role-playing. Blindfolding people, confining them to wheelchairs, or plugging their ears are just some of the ways used to disable the able, so that they can experience the role of the handicapped person. Research suggests that these simulations are only successful under certain conditions. Most importantly, the role-players must get a realistic impression of the disability and a chance to experience the reactions of strangers. Realistic simulations involving contact with strangers have been effective in producing attitude changes which were maintained up to four months later. Moreover, a partner who followed the role-player, at a distance but close enough to observe, also changed to the same extent.

Another technique of experiential learning is project work. Participants are assigned tasks which involve seeking out information and making use of it—for example, writing an essay or making a speech which espouses a strongly positive attitude. Two factors— searching out the supportive data and presenting it in public—are thought to account for the success of this method.

Experiential learning methods have been only loosely explored as means of changing attitudes. Clearly they are labour-intensive methods and are limited to small groups. Nevertheless, they have been found effective in changing people's perceptions. Moreover, the change has been relatively long-term in nature. These methods, therefore, are promising as means for changing attitudes.

8.2.3 Legislation

Legislation is surely the ultimate method of making people behave in a particular way. If they do not behave according to the law, they will be punished. This is a powerful argument when trying to make people behave contrary to their own desires. For example, it is often easier to persuade some people against drinking and driving by using the argument that it is against the law and they could lose their licence, than it is by arguing that they might injure or kill someone because their reactions are dulled. Additionally, the law provides an 'excuse' for the 'macho' to modify his behaviour.

Legislation has been seen to be effective in inducing changes in behaviour and consequently in attitudes. The commonly cited example is that of the seat-belt legislation in the U K. Another example concerns organ donation. There is a shortage of kidneys for transplantation in Britain. This may partly be a result of the reluctance of doctors to ask the relatives of suitable donors if they would be prepared to donate the kidneys. This request is often extremely difficult to make at this time of great stress and sadness for the relatives, and so doctors sometimes avoid the issue. In some American states, however, legislation has made it compulsory that the request for organ donation be made to the relatives of every suitable case. This has made it easier for the doctors to request donation (their attitudes have changed towards requesting organ donation: they are asking the favour because they *have* to do so); and it is reported that donation rates have increased by 1000 per cent.

It should be remembered that legislation can act to influence behaviour in ways other than the coercive. Legislation can be passed to support the education of the public, and can produce incentives for behaviour change, by giving encouragement to individuals and groups to change their lifestyles. Legislation can influence the way in which insurance rates are structured, and thereby provide an incentive to be a non-smoker, for example. The price and availability of foodstuffs can also be altered by legislation, and thereby encourage or inhibit healthy eating habits.

The picture is not as simple as this, however, for there are frequently powerful lobbies acting on the government against legislation facilitating healthy lifestyles. The power of the tobacco, alcohol, and sugar lobbies has been widely reported. Political and economic factors are formidable barriers to legislative action (see p. 53).

Legislation may have limited effects for other reasons too. It has been stated (Pinet 1987; p. 88) that 'little will be achieved in trying to induce behavioural changes through legal measures if public opinion has not been properly prepared. A law, even the soundest one, that does not have public support, cannot be implemented.' Pinet makes the point here that the value of particular measures needs to be understood by the population before these measures are imposed by the state. The seat-belt legislation in the UK might not have been accepted if it had not been preceded by Jimmy Savile's 'Clunk-Click' campaign to educate the public about the issue.

We can go beyond Pinet's point and argue that even if there is public support for an issue about which legislation is then passed, this may not be sufficient to induce behavioural change. It is illegal to sell cigarettes to children under the age of 16, and research in the Glasgow area has indicated much public support for this law. However, the law is constantly being violated and does not seem to be effective in preventing the sale of cigarettes to children. Some reasons for this may be suggested.

First, there is an economic incentive for selling cigarettes to children, particularly as single cigarettes. This economic interest could outweigh any gut-reaction feeling that it is an immoral practice. Secondly, the people who are selling the cigarettes may not themselves be supportive of the legislation; and may be unaffected by the widely held social attitude of disapproval. Thirdly, the police do not have the time (or perhaps the motivation) to enforce the law. These reasons do not by themselves suggest that legislation is necessarily ineffectual, but rather that the penalties are not taken sufficiently seriously.

To conclude, legislation has been effective in inducing behaviour change under certain conditions. It has been argued that a favourable environment is required for legislation to have the desired effect. Therefore, other methods for changing attitudes should be used in addition to legislation. Clearly, legislation has a permanency which ensures a longer-term change in behaviour than do other methods. However, legislation is limited (to a greater extent than are other methods) by the prevailing political and economic environments. The moral justification for health legislation will be considered in Chapter 10.

8.3 Conclusions

1. The chapter has reviewed many of the ways in which attitudes can be changed. Recommendations have been made concerning ways of increasing the effectiveness of these methods in changing attitudes, and workers in the field are likely to raise their chances of success by noting the type of recommendations made.

2. It is never possible to guarantee success in changing attitudes, however, as there are often many factors resisting change. Deep-seated attitudes tend to be part of an integrated pattern of associated beliefs, and so it is extremely difficult to change them item by item. Moreover, many attitudes are a function of society or group membership, rather than of the isolated individual. The power of group membership is important, particularly regarding conformity and obedience/allegiance to the group.

3. Attempts to alter attitudes may simply result in the 'recipient' mustering his or her defences and becoming all the more entrenched in the original beliefs.

4. There are no watertight methods for changing attitudes, and progress will be made only in small steps. Research, however, is showing us how we can ensure that those steps will be in the right direction.

9 Values

In Chapter 7 we discussed the nature of attitudes and the various ways in which they may be changed. This immediately raises the question of the direction in which they ought to be changed. In other words, it raises the question of values. The question of values in the context of health promotion is complex. We shall try to analyse the nature of values and valuing, the nature of the values which are necessary if an individual person and a society are going to flourish, and the bearing which the activities of health promotion have on these values. These questions, which are often glossed over in the literature, are of the first importance for a proper understanding and justification of health promotion, as we stressed in our account of health in Chapter 2.

9.1 Terminology

One of the difficulties in the literature of health education and health promotion is that terminology varies. We have already encountered this in the discussions in Part 1. Terminology for discussing values is particularly varied. This is partly because health promotion is an eclectic discipline which draws from a range of social sciences, from health care sciences of all kinds, from traditional moral philosophy, and from lay perceptions. It is also partly because health promotion is attempting to forge its own concepts to express its own distinctive insights.

Sometimes this confusion is a simple matter of new words for old ideas. For example, we shall speak here mainly of 'self-development' where we have previously stressed the importance of 'acquiring lifeskills'; and in this chapter we shall stick to the traditional emphasis on the importance of developing 'autonomy' whereas we previously spoke of the importance of 'empowerment'. We therefore ask our readers to consider whether the terminology which comes easily from their own professional approach can be translated into this terminology without loss. In a new and rapidly developing discipline it is important to be tolerant of a variety of approaches and terminology.

Confusion can also extend beyond terminology to the values which lie behind it. Once again, the fact that several currents of thought and concern flow into health promotion is important. For example, the medical values of public health, and the educational values of traditional health education, mingle with newer values of consumerism and 'getting the message across'. We shall try to clarify the value stance of health promotion in this chapter and the next, and we shall try to clarify the political stance of health promotion in Chapter 11. In attempting to do this we shall no doubt express our own moral and political position, but we shall try to show that the moral and political values of health promotion derive from its intrinsic *professional* concerns rather than from any extraneous non-professional reasons.

The word 'ethics' is more familiar in the wider literature of health care than 'values', so the question arises as to why we are making the term 'values' central. The term 'ethics', despite its frequent use, has no clear or consistent use in the literature of health care (Downie and Calman 1987) but it is sometimes used to refer to the first-order problems which are encountered in the practice of health care. We shall use the terms 'value' and 'value-judgement' here rather than either 'ethics' and 'ethical judgement' or 'morals' and 'moral judgement'. There are three reasons for preferring this usage.

First, it brings out the continuity between the value dilemmas encountered in ordinary life and those dealt with in the professional practice of health promotion. The point here is that the activity of health promotion is one which can be approached from numerous professional standpoints, such as medicine, dentistry, nursing, education, and social work. What these various professionals have in common, and can bring to health promotion, is their sense of judgement as ordinary human beings informed and sensitized by their professional backgrounds. Certainly, there is a growing knowledge-base to health promotion, but it is vital that health promotion should not develop as a new kind of esoteric expertise divorced from the values and ideas implicit in lay perceptions of health and a good life. If we think in this way of health promotion, as an activity of 'enabling', 'articulating', 'crystallizing' or 'refining and mobilizing' the values implicit in lay perceptions, or of 'empowering' individuals, then it is preferable to use terms which emphasize the continuity with ordinary situations. We are therefore proposing to speak of 'values' rather than 'ethics'.

A second reason for preferring the term 'values' to 'ethics' is that it emphasizes the essentially contestable nature of the practice of health promotion. The term 'ethics', especially in the context of medical ethics, is apt to suggest the unchangeable principles of hallowed tradition; a body of rules written on tablets of stone by the Greeks, and nowadays developed by committees of 'experts'. But this spirit is quite alien to the practice of health promotion. Public involvement and debate are essential in all areas of health promotion, and a 'top-down' approach is undesirable. To use the term 'values' rather than 'ethics' is to suggest that differences of approach and emphasis are desirable.

Thirdly, the term 'values' brings out much more clearly than the term 'ethics' the breadth of the problems involved. For example, in Chapter 10 we shall raise as a problem of values the priority which should be given to individual freedom when that is an obstacle to community health. Clearly, such a problem is wider than anything conceived within the framework of professional ethics. Again, we consider, in various contexts, concepts such as self-development or social justice. Discussion of such concepts involves information which derives from a range of social sciences, but it also involves value-judgements, although perhaps not 'ethical judgements' in the narrow sense.

In summary, we can say that while specialist health promoters may in time develop a code of ethics to regulate their professional practices, it is preferable to think of their activities as being essentially concerned with values and value-judgements. This is because the term 'values' brings out the continuity between the work of health promoters and our own ordinary judgements of good and bad forms of individual and social life; it brings out the essentially contestable nature of the activities of health promoters and therefore the importance of public participation in the debate about values; and it brings out the breadth of the value-base of health promotion. We must also be alert to the wide variety of terms, professional and lay, which are used to express values.

9.2 What are values?

To answer this question we may consider first what kinds of thing are naturally spoken of as a person's values (Downie and Telfer

1980). We say, for example, 'My values (or 'my values in life') are integrity, kindness, beauty'. Does this just mean: 'These are the things I value?' No, because I may value highly my car or my hiking boots, but it would be odd to say that these things were among my values, except as a joke.

This is not a moral point about the triviality of having such things as one's values. Rather it is a conceptual point about a person's values. In the case of a car or hiking boots, we can always ask why someone sets such a high value on such things, and get an answer in terms of more general considerations. For example, a woman may say she values her car because it gives her freedom or excitement, and she may value her hiking boots because they are comfortable. But where something is to be regarded as among a person's values, no further reason can be given why these things are valued. If kindness is among a person's values then it is valued for its own sake, and other things (e.g. a thoughtful letter) can be valued as exemplifying the fundamental value.

Can we then say that a person's values are simply those things which are valued *for their own sake*? This is not very informative without further discussion of what it is to value something. Now, a great deal has been written on this, but a fairly rough-and-ready characterization will do for our present purposes. We might try the approach that valuing is to do with preference and choice; to value something more highly than something else is to choose to have it or get it in preference to the other thing, to choose to hold on to it in preference to the other thing, and so on.

Described in this way valuing is essentially comparative—we value by comparing and then choosing—whereas simply having certain values does not seem to be so. But we can accommodate the apparent non-comparativeness of what are said to be a person's values in terms of the comparative notion by saying that a person's values are those things which for their own sakes are preferred to everything else. Thus, if health is among a person's values, he or she will sacrifice other things in order to achieve health, unless another value is also at stake or the person is weak-willed.

But this account of valuing fails to distinguish between two distinct ways in which something might be valued for its own sake. The distinction is best explained by means of an example. Suppose an independent, elderly man takes a lot of pains to live on his own, sacrificing all sorts of possibilities in order to maintain this independence, apparently with no further end in view—we would then say that independence is one of his values. Now there are two possibilities. On the one hand, he may say that he happens to like independence but is happy to let others stay with relatives or enter institutions. On the other hand, he may disapprove of those who depend on others, and try to bring up his children to set the same store by independence as he does himself. Again, a man who values thrift and enterprise for their own sakes may either simply like to be thrifty and enterprising, as a matter of temperament; or he may approve of thrift and enterprise in himself and others, be ashamed of himself if he is extravagant or unenterprising, and so on. We can call the first kind of values 'liking values' (though liking will be too mild a word to convey the strength of some valuings of this kind), and the second kind 'moral values'. When people speak of values they more often mean moral values, and if we use the word 'values' without qualification we shall be referring to moral values.

Both liking values and moral values affect people's conduct; they lead them to act, inspire their conduct, and have a bearing on their attitudes, as we saw in Chapter 7. But moral values, as distinct from liking values, have an interpersonal quality. People with a particular moral value will judge others as well as themselves in terms of it. That is the source of the attitudes of approval and disapproval which are characteristic expressions of moral values. We shall later consider (Section 10.3) whether 'health' is a liking value or a moral value.

We are now in a position to raise the question of the relationship between values and attitudes. The answer is that values—both liking and moral values—are subsets of attitudes. Attitudes, we said, have cognitive, affective, and conative components. The same is true of values, which are expressed in *behaviour*, and through *preferences* based on *beliefs* about objects, persons, or situations, and are accompanied by *feelings* of approval or disapproval. For example, some individuals may judge that conduct likely to risk the spread of AIDS is wrong. This means that they choose one mode of behaviour rather than other because they entertain certain beliefs about the spread of AIDS and the harm it may cause themselves or others, that they disapprove of others who act in high-risk ways, and feel guilty if they themselves do so. In other words, having a value is the very same as having a certain sort of attitude.

Values, then, are preferences which both express attitudes and affect attitudes. The relationship may be conveyed as follows:

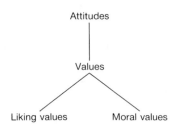

9.3 Necessary social values

It is often maintained that values differ enormously in different societies and in different parts of the same society. This view is sometimes expressed by saying that values are 'relative' to a society, or, even more drastically, that they are 'subjective' and personal to the people holding them. We wish to argue that this view is exaggerated. Whereas some values have changed historically, and there are differences over many values in different areas of contemporary society, there are also other values which are widely shared, and indeed *must* be widely shared for the continuance of society. There are other values again which are necessary for individual human flourishing. We shall consider the latter in Section 9.4, but let us begin by considering the sense in which some values must be adopted or accepted, or must develop, in any continuing society. These we regard as consensus values, and they are the very same as those which constitute the collective dimension of the social well-being of the WHO definition discussed in Chapter 2.

One approach to the idea of consensus values is to describe in general terms the human predicament for which the existence of consensus values is the partial solution. The description of human nature and its predicament we shall give will consist of a few obvious truths about human nature. Such a description brings out the close links between the kind of nature we have and the kind of values we have. To say this is not say that values can be deduced from the facts of human nature, but rather that we accept the kind of values we do because we are the kind of people we are, that any plausible account of values must have close links with an account of what people and their environment are like. It will emerge that because people and their environment have certain characteristics, obvious to us all, they must observe certain rules or constraints on their behaviour— or not survive. In other words, we are assuming that whatever may be the full analysis of consensus values, they at least give rise to principles which help us to live together more harmoniously and co-operatively than we otherwise would without such principles. To say this is not to deny that values may have a spiritual dimension, but it is to assert that they have a social function, and that we have an interest in accepting certain principles of behaviour.

As a first example of how an obvious fact about human beings gives rise to principles of behaviour let us note that human beings have bodies and minds which are vulnerable both to attack and disease, and are easily damaged by either. This obvious physical fact, which we examined in detail in Chapter 2, is the basis of the values of physical integrity and health and the disvalues expressed in concepts like 'assault' or 'illness'. These values give rise to rules and customs, found in any society, which restrict the use of physical violence in social life and minimize the risk of disease. A concept like 'assault' logically could not exist unless the human body were liable to physical damage. And, in more general terms, a principle such as 'One ought not to harm', or 'One ought to help people in distress', clearly reflect the facts that people are liable to injury and are vulnerable physically to deliberate attacks, accidental mishaps, and diseases.

Less obviously, but just as importantly for our purposes, human beings are vulnerable to psychological pressures of all sorts. Sometimes these may be inflicted by social forces, such as economic constraints. This obvious fact lies behind many of the campaigns for social justice, for the constant threat or reality of poverty damages human beings. The human psyche is vulnerable also to damage from gossip or patronizing behaviour, or to self-inflicted feelings of guilt or inadequacy. As we shall see, such obvious facts about human beings lie behind many of our basic values as to how people should be treated in society. For example, the health promoter's stress on building up self-esteem reflects such facts. Indeed, health promotion in general, as we stressed in Chapters 2–4 is concerned with facilitating true well-being in adverse physical and social circumstances.

Secondly, human needs and wants can more adequately be satisfied co-operatively by division of labour, than by each fending for himself. These facts are reflected in the complexities of social and economic organization, with its value of justice, which we shall discuss in Chapter 11. Other concepts important for health promotion, such as 'neighbourliness', 'citizenship' and 'self-help', can also be seen to reflect basic human needs and wants.

Thirdly, human beings are approximately equal in most respects. Some people are stronger or cleverer or more attractive than others, but on the whole these natural gifts tend to balance out, giving us all an interest in accepting principles which work for the benefit of all.

Fourthly, human rationality is limited, and rules are therefore helpful to guide us on the likely consequence of action. J.S. Mill (1861) said that rules are like signposts which guide us when we are not sure where to go, or they distil the wisdom of mankind on the consequences of action.

Fifthly, human sympathy exists—by nature we have the germs of benevolence or compassion within us—but our benevolence is limited and easily swamped by the stronger natural endowment of self-assertion in all its forms. We recognize this in each other and therefore have an interest in belonging to a system of morality the principles of which correct our bias towards self-interest.

Finally, the resources of the environment are scarce and require work for their production and distribution through service industries. Scarcity gives us an interest in property and in the many rules of justice for the legitimate ownership and fair transfer of property and other goods and services, including health care.

These six facts put together explain why we have an *interest* in accepting a system of social values or why a consensus is desirable. For it seems to follow from such obvious natural facts that, on the whole, we will all do better for ourselves by belonging to a system of organization which reflects the consensus values. Of course, not everyone accepts those values, and changing circumstances modify them, but a majority accept them. This is especially so when the values are enshrined and safeguarded by a system of law and legal sanctions.

The most basic of these principles which derive from what we have called 'consensus values' are the following:

1. One ought not to harm other people physically or psychologically (non-maleficence).

2. One ought to give positive help to people wherever necessary (benevolence or beneficence, and compassion).

3. One ought to treat people fairly or equally before the law, in the ownership and transfer of goods and services, rewarding labour, and in general in determining social conditions (justice).

4. One ought to produce the best possible consequences (or the greatest happiness) for the majority (utility).

These values can all be seen to be acceptable to human beings, granted the limitations already mentioned of human nature and the human situation. And of course these four consensus values will give rise to many detailed rules of helping others—property rules, rules of fair dealing, and many more. In the next two chapters we shall consider how these values and principles of social life are or ought to be the guiding principles or 'ethics' of health promotion in various social, personal, and educational contexts. In other words, if these are the values which constitute societal well-being, they must also be the values which health promotion is attempting to nurture.

9.4 Necessary individual or personal values

Let us now turn from social values to individual or personal values. Again, just as we maintained that there are some social values which must be widely shared if societies are going to operate on a harmonious and co-operative basis, so we maintain that there are some individual and personal values which are necessary for a good, in the sense of flourishing, individual human life. Once again, the fruitful question is not 'What values do individuals in fact have?' but rather, 'What are the values which are components of a flourishing human life?'

One important and widely shared personal value can be called the ability to be self-determining, the ability to be able to choose for oneself or, more extensively, to be able to formulate and carry out one's own plans or policies. The importance we attach to these abilities is reflected in our approval of traits of character such as 'being able to stand on one's own feet', 'knowing what one wants', 'having aims in one's life', or 'being able to make up one's own mind'. The connection between developing such traits of character and being a person is reflected in theories of education which stress the importance of cultivating such dispositions in children. Conversely, to impair a person's abilities to formulate and carry out aims and policies of his or her own devising is to that extent to injure him or her as a person. For example, if a person has been injured physically or mentally there is often a tendency for friends to offer too much help, for it is often easier to do something for people than to wait patiently while they try to do it for themselves; and this ease and convenience can assume the guise of kindness. But it may be a subtle way of eroding someone's nature as a person. The development of personality can also be blocked in grander ways by political arrangements which restrict the images people can form of themselves, or by consumer societies which impose certain images of people. Self-determination, then, is a personal value essential to the growth and development of the human personality and therefore to true well-being (Downie and Telfer 1980).

A second value which is important for the integrity and flourishing of human personality we can call the ability to be self-governing. Philosophers such as Kant have attached great importance to this value, and have certainly exaggerated the extent to which it can actually be realized in most people's lifestyle, granted the many economic and psychological pressures on them in their everyday lives. Nevertheless, it is correct to say that the ability to be detached, to stand back from one's own self-interest, to take account of the needs of others as well as of one's own—in short, mould one's conduct in terms of values applying to all equally—is one mark of the mature personality.

A third value to which individuals attach a great deal of importance, and which is necessary for a mature personality, we can call a sense of responsibility. Human beings assume that they are responsible for their actions, unless in some way they are compelled to act as they do, or they do not understand what they are doing. Approaches to human beings which ignore or deny this factor, such as some medical, psychiatric, or social work interventions, can be experienced as patronizing and an affront to human dignity.

A fourth personal value to which people attach importance we can identify in general terms as self-development or self-realization. Most people feel that there are some activities—physical, mental, social—which they are or could be good at. This awareness goes along with a desire to develop the capacity or express it. Sometimes this may take the form of what we have earlier called a 'liking value'. For instance, some people have a capacity for a sport, and they wish to develop this or express it by actually playing. At other times the awareness of this capacity may take the stronger form of what we have called a moral value; some people feel that it is morally incumbent on them to develop their gifts for their own sake and not because the gifts may be useful to others. An example of this is the person of mature years who leaves a job in order to begin a course of full-time study which will not necessarily lead to a better job but may lead to self-development and thereby improved self-esteem. That this preference is a moral value, and not just a liking value, is indicated by the fact that sometimes a person will feel justified in sacrificing the interests of family or friends for it. In other words, a desire for self-development can at times outweigh a social value. We shall later consider the relationship between health and self-development.

Some philosophers deny that there can be a self-regarding side to morality, such as we are identifying via the concept of self-development. They see morality as having an essentially social function, concerned only with regulating one's conduct *vis-à-vis* other members of society. Such a view has developed out of one strand in J. S. Mill's thinking. Mill (1859) in his essay *On Liberty* seemed to be arguing that moral issues arise only to the extent that one's conduct harms other people; in so far as one's conduct affects only oneself it does not raise a moral issue. Yet in the same essay Mill has a chapter on 'self-development', in which he does not seem to regard it as a matter of moral indifference what kind of person one is. As he puts it (in his Chapter 3): 'It really is of importance not only what men do, but also what manner of men they are that do it.' And this view, that there are moral duties to cultivate in oneself certain characteristic human excellences, goes back to Plato and Aristotle, and is taken up in a slightly different form by the Judaeo-Christian tradition. In other words, self-development has been regarded as a morally important attitude from the earliest.

We have already noted in this chapter that there can be alternative terms for the same concept. The literature on health education and health promotion recognizes the importance of what we have called 'self-development' by its stress on the importance of acquiring 'lifeskills'. In particular, lifeskills involve learning how to make decisions, to take control of one's own life, rather than be at the mercy of circumstances (see pp. 30, 35). Other writers (Antonovsky 1984) stress the importance of acquiring a 'sense of coherence' in one's life. These and no doubt others are overlapping terms for what we are identifying as 'self-development'.

It might be objected that we have said little in this chapter about self-esteem, a concept much stressed in the health promotion literature. But self-esteem is not a value in its own right because it cannot be chosen. What can be chosen is self-development, or, in more typical health promotion language, the development of lifeskills. Now if a person chooses to develop lifeskills then self-esteem will result. In other words, self-esteem is a by-product of lifeskills. It is a sign that self-development is going well, rather than an aim.

9.5 Autonomy

These four values—self-determination, self-government, sense of responsibility, and self-development—are clearly linked. For example, self-development will often be achieved by exercising self-determination. In other words, we develop the self by achieving certain purposes or acquiring lifeskills. Again, people often feel responsible for their failure to develop their gifts and blame themselves. In view of the overlapping and connected nature of these personal values it is helpful to regard them all as being different aspects of a single concept—autonomy. The concept of autonomy is often used in the literature of medical, nursing, and social work ethics, but less commonly analysed. We are suggesting that it encapsulates the four important personal values of self-determination, self-government, sense of responsibility,.and self-development.

It is important to make three further points about the autonomous person, as we understand the value of autonomy. The first is that we are not excluding as unimportant human emotions and desires. It will be remembered that we have maintained that values are a subset of attitudes. They have therefore a cognitive, an affective, and a conative component. In so far as autonomy is the unifying value of individual personality it too will have all three aspects, and thus will have an affective aspect.

The second point which must be stressed about the autonomous person is that he or she is a kind of abstraction from a social situation. Human beings do not exist in complete separation from each other. The ingredients of autonomy all carry an essential reference to society. Our self-determination, self-government, sense of responsibility, and self-development are not only emotionally charged but also exist only in a social context and cannot really be understood without that dimension. The autonomous self is a social self.

Politically this means that the autonomous person is a citizen—his or her nature and values cannot be understood outside a political and economic framework. Emotionally it means that the autonomous person does not live in a vacuum; persons exist in emotional relationships with others and these relationships are essential to their identity. As we shall show in the next two chapters, there are messages to be learned from this for health promotion.

The third point, which is made many times in this book, is that autonomy is a *value*, an ideal to be aimed at rather than a characteristic which everyone possesses. People are frequently prevented—by social and economic forces, by pressures from commercial interests or peer groups—from developing their capacity for autonomy. Health promotion is one movement which contributes to the development of autonomy. That is why health promoters often express their professional aims in terms of the concept of empowerment. To empower people is to enable them to develop their autonomy, or to 'be all they can be'. This was a central theme of Chapters 2–4.

9.6 Linking social and personal values

From the point of view of our theory of values there is a parallel between social values—the values necessary for the flourishing of society—and individual values, those necessary for the flourishing of the individual personality. It is common in social and political philosophy to depict social values as laying claims upon us, but to depict individual values as being at best 'liking values'—matters of arbitrary preference. Our view is that individual values impose claims on us also. In the case of social values the constraints which make the values *claims*, rather than just *likings*, are the threats of disharmonious and unco-operative social relationships. Analogously, the constraints which make individual values claims are the threats of disharmony and disintegration within the self. Liberal philosophy characteristically stresses the values of avoiding harm to others, and suggests, more or less explicitly, that the self is a structureless receptacle for indiscriminate satisfaction. We, on the contrary, hold that the self has a structure just as society has, and that a sense of coherence and self-esteem, and therefore of true well-being, come from the awareness that the personal values we have mentioned are being expressed in a way of life.

The parallel between social and individual values establishes a link but only a weak link between them. Is there any other way of linking them? Kant sees individual and social values as being two aspects of a single principle, which he expresses as: 'Respect the autonomous nature of human beings whether in your own person or in that of another' (Kant 1782).

It is important to stress that Kant thought of it as an obligation to develop in ourselves the qualities which make us distinctively human beings. Most liberal writers are inclined to state the Kantian slogan as: Respect for persons. The implicit suggestion of the abbreviated formula is that it is only *other* persons which are meant. But we are following Kant in thinking that our own personality lays claims upon us; there is a duty to 'be all we can be'.

These basic values can be indicated and linked as shown in the diagram below.

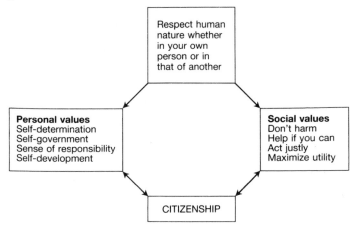

9.7 Conclusions

1. An examination of values is of importance for health promotion because health promotion is concerned with changing attitudes. The justification for this project clearly involves pervasive value judgements about desirable lifestyles.

2. Values are either 'liking values' or 'moral values' but in either case they are expressions of attitudes and as such have cognitive, affective, and conative components.

3. There are certain consensus values which societies must adopt if they are to flourish. These are the values of inter-personal relationships. Other values are necessary for individual human flourishing. In both cases the values are the expression of obvious physical or psychological truths about human beings and the constraints on their lives, and in both cases the values are the source of the empowerment which constitutes true societal and individual well-being.

10 Liberalism, autonomy, and health

We have discussed in our previous chapter what it is to value something, and have identified the values which are necessary for individual and social flourishing. In this and the next chapter we shall discuss the methods by which health promotion attempts to further the values of autonomy and social justice which we have identified as being necessary for the flourishing of the individual and society. Here it is helpful to state the five principles which WHO (1984) sees as the basis of health promotion.

1. Health promotion involves the population as a whole in the context of their everyday life, rather than focusing on people at risk for specific diseases.

2. Health promotion is directed towards action on the causes or determinants of health.

3. Health promotion combines diverse, but complementary, methods or approaches, including communication, education, legislation, fiscal measures, organizational change, community development, and spontaneous local activities against health hazards.

4. Health promotion aims particularly at effective and concrete public participation.

5. While health promotion is basically an activity in the health and social fields, and not a medical service, health professionals—particularly in primary health care—have an important role in nurturing and enabling health promotion.

We shall try to show in this and the next chapter how these principles can be used to further the values which are essential components of health. In this chapter we shall concentrate mainly on the way they can be used for the enhancement of individual autonomy, and in Chapter 11 we shall consider ways in which they relate to social justice.

It is clear from our view of the place of values in health promotion that we regard it as strongly normative. But not all of those engaged in health promotion share our view that the activity is value-driven. Before considering the way in which health promotion encourages the growth of certain values we must therefore defend our view that health promotion is not a neutral activity. Let us begin by examining the process known in health promotion as 'value(s)-clarification'. This will also assist in further explaining our position on the value-base of health promotion.

10.1 Values-clarification

The term 'values-clarification' refers to processes by which persons or groups can be assisted in finding out what their values really are. There are various methods which can be used to bring about a clarification of this kind (Ewles and Simnett 1985). For example, people might be encouraged to write down and rank the activities they enjoy, or they might be asked to state the arguments in favour of something they feel strongly about. Again, role-play or games may be used to encourage groups to become clear on their values. Now, the details of these procedures are very important for practical purposes, but we are more interested in the principles and assumptions behind them.

Ewles and Simnett (p. 132) write as follows: 'Traditional teaching operates in the hope that the "right" attitudes and values will be "caught" by learners. In contrast, we suggest that health education requires people to think critically about their values and build up their own value system.' Social work literature in a similar vein suggests that in dealing with clients it is important to be 'non-judgemental' (Downie and Telfer 1980). Now, if the assumption here is that any set of values is as good as any other then it is not an assumption which is consistent with health education or promotion, or indeed any sort of education whatsoever. Certainly, it is important that people should be encouraged to think critically about their values, and although our predecessors in health education did not have such imaginative methods as are nowadays recommended for values-clarification there is no reason to think that the encouragement of critical appraisal has not always been part of health education. What does need to be questioned however is the phrase 'build up their own value system' and the correlative idea of the non-judgemental attitude.

We are attempting to bring out in the chapters on values that health education and other aspects of health promotion are activities committed to certain views on the nature of the self and what makes it flourish, and to views of a well-ordered society. No doubt there are a large number of acceptable ways of living one's life, all of which lead to the flourishing of human personality, but not *every* way is acceptable. Similarly, there are no doubt several acceptable forms of social and political organization, but not *every* way is acceptable to those involved in health promotion. If these positions are not shared by health educators and health promoters, then why adopt slogans such as 'Be all you can be', or why deplore the 'health divide'? In other words, health promoters cannot consistently accept the 'sneer' quotes in Ewles and Simnett's phrase ' "right" attitudes', for health promoters must believe that there are right attitudes to the individual and to society, or go out of business.

It is a totally different point what methods or procedures should be adopted to change attitudes in individuals or societies. Consider this analogy. A Christian missionary priest is not likely to be very successful if he arrives among a heathen tribe and declares 'All have sinned!'. He may be committed to believing this, but he would be well-advised to live and work among the people and learn about their ways of life and their difficulties before he tries to change their attitudes. In a similar way, it might be counter-productive to preach too much about giving up smoking or going to the pub every night; but, all the same, a health promoter is committed to the view that smoking and heavy drinking are objectively bad. Again, there may be some doubt as to whether jogging is a desirable form of exercise in all, or indeed in any, circumstances, but there can be no doubt that taking regular exercise is objectively a good form of activity and should be part of a good life. In the area of political values, there can be room for difference of opinion about the relative importance of values such as liberty and equality—we shall discuss this later—but health promoters are surely committed to the view that a large health divide between rich and poor is wrong. But it is a different question of political tactics how this state of affairs is best changed.

Consider this example, again from Ewles and Simnett. In discussing the inadequacies of traditional health education (p. 32) they state that it has sometimes involved (among other failings):

. . . the imposition of medical values on the client. Frequently, this means the imposition of middle-class values on working-class people, and the ethical justification for this is doubtful. For example, losing weight and

lowering blood pressure may be the most important thing to a doctor, but
drinking beer in the pub with friends may be far more important to his
overweight, middle-aged, unemployed patient. Who is to say which set of
values is 'right'—the doctor or his patient? Whose life is it anyway?

Two points can be made here. First, if the client wants to lose
weight then he ought to take the doctor's advice and cut down on his
beer drinking. Otherwise, why consult the doctor at all? Secondly,
the health promoter is presumably committed to believing that
health is at least one important value, and so is also committed to
believing that the client should try to take the doctor's advice. It is a
totally different question how the health promoter should go about
persuading someone to do this. That question is one of method, on
which Ewles and Simnett have many excellent points to make. But if
every set of values is as good as every other, then health promoters
might as well pack up and go home. It is surely the belief that there
are better and worse ways of living one's life that makes the whole
practice of health education, promotion, social work, nursing, and
medicine worthwhile.

To sum up what we consider to be the underlying principles of
values-clarification, we are maintaining three principles: that it is
important to encourage people to clarify their own values; that the
methods used in doing this should be flexible and imaginative; that
health promoters are committed by their profession to believing that
there are right and wrong attitudes to life and its values.

10.2 Assumptions of liberalism

In our previous chapter we identified the values which are necessary
for the flourishing of individuals and societies. But health promotion takes place in a specific cultural context with assumptions specific to the context about how life should be lived. The framework of
values to be found in Britain and the rest of Western Europe, North
America, Australasia, and other areas influenced by these can be
defined economically, politically, and morally. Economically, this
outlook is expressed in some form of free market economy; politically it is expressed in some form of representative democracy; and
morally it is expressed in some form of what is called the 'harm
principle'—that individuals have a right to act as they want unless
they are harming others. (This is often what is meant by 'freedom'.)
Taken together these strands can conveniently be labelled 'liber-

alism' or 'liberal democracy', and they constitute one, but only one, historical embodiment of the values we have identified as necessary for individual and social flourishing.

One important current of thought leading to the modification of some of these assumptions of the liberal outlook is health promotion. In this and the next chapter we shall be discussing the impact of health promotion on liberal ideas. What are the assumptions of the liberal outlook, at least as it applies to health? We shall list the assumptions and then go on to criticize or at least to modify them in the light of the values of health promotion. The liberal position on the pursuit of health assumes the following:

1. A view of health as an instrumental or enabling value, and as not making a claim as a positive value in its own right.

2. The view that people have a right to pursue their own health but no duty to do so unless their ill-health is harming others, this view being thought to be an expression of autonomy, or the 'harm principle'.

3. The connected view that the government has no duty to safeguard or enhance health other than through the prevention of harm.

4. A negative view of health legislation, as restricting autonomy in the interests of health.

5. A negative view of autonomy, that you have it to the extent that you are not prevented from doing what you want to do.

6. An atomistic view of society, that it consists of associations of individuals linked by a common geography, system of government, and economic ties.

Some of these assumptions are definitive of liberalism, and others are views which tend to go along with it in the context of health care. Together they constitute the bare bones of a coherent philosophy of health care and much besides.

Nevertheless, there are ideas in the contemporary consciousness which lead people to question these assumptions. Out of these ideas a point of view can be developed which challenges classical liberalism. Some of these ideas go back to the Beveridge Report, or earlier to late nineteenth century 'citizenship' movements (Vincent and Plant 1984). But others spring from new movements of thought on the nature of health and how it should be pursued. All are to be found at least in vague form in contemporary social attitudes, and we shall develop them by means of a critique of liberalism which derives from our conception of citizenship.

10.3 Health as a value

The first assumption of the liberal position on health and health care is that health is not a positive value in its own right, but simply a means to attain other values. Health promotion, particularly in its emphasis on positive health—on being all you can be—must reject the first liberal assumption. But it might be objected that just to assume that health is a value in its own right is simply to express the over-enthusiasm of health promoters. Our book is concerned with basic principles and we must therefore try to *establish* that health is indeed a value in its own right. When that is done it will then be appropriate to consider what sort of value it is.

It will be remembered that we argued that the idea of a value is best approached from the point of view of the activity of valuing. To value something, we said, is to choose it for its own sake in preference to other alternatives. Now, it is not immediately obvious that health fits this account, for two reasons. It might be argued, first, that one does not choose health at all, one either has it or does not have it. And it might be argued, secondly, that even if there is a sense in which one can choose health, it is not chosen for its own sake, but for the sake of the values which cannot be attained without it. This expresses the liberal assumption we are presently discussing.

The first point is valid but not fundamental. It is true that one cannot exactly choose health in the way in which one can choose new clothes. But 'choosing health' is just a shorthand way of speaking of choosing goods and lifestyles which are likely to conduce to or enhance health.

The second point again is valid but not the whole truth. It is valid in that health is certainly an instrumental value, and may be chosen for that reason. This is true whether we are thinking in terms of the individual or of society. To see health in this way is to see it in utilitarian terms. If a society is going to flourish then its members must be healthy. There is therefore a utilitarian justification—a justification in terms of health economics—for a government to promote health. Equally, in the life of the individual, the possession of health is a necessary condition of the attainment of other goods. To describe health as an instrumental value with utilitarian justification is not of course to suggest that it is unimportant. Even if health were simply a means to others' ends it would still be of the first importance, granted that it is a means or a necessary condition for so many other individual and social values. In other words, what we have listed as the first assumption of liberalism about health and health care is correct in its first part.

But there are limitations to this approach to health. First, it depicts health as being good simply for what it brings, whereas it is more plausible to argue that health is also good for what it is. In other words, health is not only an instrumental value, but a value in its own right. Secondly, if health were simply an instrumental value, there would be limits to reasonable governmental promotion of health. In other words, the political justification for promoting health would need to be in terms of preventing ill-health, or promoting functional health in the sense of the ability to carry on a job and not be a drain on resources. But we wish to claim that the government does have a duty to promote health in the positive sense. We must therefore, as a first step, argue that health is a value in its own right. We shall argue for the second step—that health is a value governments should promote—in Section 10.5. How can the case for the first step be made out?

One obvious reason for valuing health for its own sake is that disease, illness, sickness, or disability are likely to be painful or unpleasant, whereas there are positive pleasures, glows of fitness and so on, which accompany the peak of health, and a sense of well-being accompanying more ordinary good health. We have discussed this in Chapter 2. Satisfactions of this kind are values in that they are desired for their own sake.

This argument is acceptable, but its scope is limited since not all forms of the absence of health are painful, even in a wide sense of 'painful' which includes 'uncomfortable' or 'distressing'. Moreover, if health is valued in this way, in terms of pleasure and the absence of pain, it is being regarded merely as a 'liking value', not as something to be approved of and recommended, and as making a reasonable claim on government support. We have seen that health is an instrumental value with social and individual utility, and that it is a 'liking value'. Our question now is whether it can be seen as an ideal or moral value, in such a way that people who cherish health are to be approved of and people who squander it are to be disapproved of. To put it another way, we can refer to Aristotle who distinguished three types of thing which people desire:

the useful, the pleasant, and the noble. It is easy to explain, as we have done, how health can be desired under the first two headings and we shall now try to explain how it can be desired under the third, as an ideal value (Downie and Telfer 1980; p. 26).

To see health as an ideal value is to have a biological or purposive idea of how our species is 'meant' to be. There are various ways of explaining this purposive idea. One way might be in terms of a wise and good God whose creative blueprint we should try to exemplify as far as possible, from whom we hold our bodies and minds in trust, and to whom we have a duty to keep them in good repair. It is worth noting, however, that a religious approach to health does not necessarily produce this conclusion. There are some strands in religious thinking in terms of which the body is depicted as evil, and the flesh as something to be mortified rather than preserved. From this point of view, a believer might thank God for his ill-health as something which keeps him from evil. But there is more characteristically a strong strain of the importance of healing the body and mind in religious thought, and that strain provides a religious justification for seeing health as an ideal value.

A second approach might be a secular one in terms of respect for the species; it might be said that it is incumbent on us as human beings to make our human nature flourish. This is an idea which goes back to Plato and has perennial appeal. J.S. Mill (1859; Chapter 3) states it as follows:

Human nature is not a machine to be built after a model, and set to do exactly the work prescribed for it, but a tree, which requires to grow and develop on all sides according to the tendency of the inward forces which make it a living thing.

This passage brings out the biological idea that health as such, apart from its usefulness and its pleasantness, is a value in its own right. The idea is certainly a source of strong feeling in many people, and it is common to hear disapproval of those who are thought to be ruining their health gratuitously.

A third source of the idea that health is a value involves an aesthetic view of health. This view is connected with the biological one, and can be connected also with the religious one. In terms of this approach, health is an ideal design with which we should try to make our bodies conform, and in terms of which aberrations are seen as ugly. People can dislike conditions in themselves and see them as ugly simply because they see them as unhealthy. We discussed this in Chapter 2. A subset of this idea connects health with other qualities which call forth human admiration, such as energy. People are approved of for being like a 'dynamo' and pulsating with energy, although they can also be approved of for being calm where that derives from control rather than passivity. These are mixtures of biological and aesthetic ideas but certainly present health as a positive value. There are then various overlapping ways of describing health in terms of which it can be seen as a value to be approved of, as well as found useful.

It might be objected to our claim that health is a value in its own right that, on the contrary, it makes for egocentricity and obsession with one's own bodily states. It might be compared to the spiritual self-absorption characteristic of some religious fanatics in earlier ages. In replying to this objection we must concede that an undue concern with physical health is a characteristic to be found in some present-day societies, perhaps especially on the west coast of the United States. But to see health as a positive good is not necessarily to commit oneself to self-absorption. It is certainly the view of the WHO that positive health is 'seen as a resource for everyday life, not the objective of living'. The point is that positive health is a value, not the supreme value. It makes perfectly good sense to weigh health against other values, and sometimes it will be reasonable to give precedence to health and sometimes not. For example, someone with a stressful lifestyle might give up a job—perhaps at some personal economic cost or even to the detriment of service to others —on the grounds that his or her health was suffering. Equally, someone might reasonably sacrifice health for another value, such as dedication to a life of scholarship or service to others. To say that health is a value and makes a claim is by no means to say it is the supreme value or requires self-absorption.

10.4 Autonomy and health

Assuming that health is a value in its own right (and that the first assumption of liberalism can therefore be rejected), we shall turn to the second assumption of the liberal position—that people have a right to pursue their own health but no duty to do so unless their ill-health is harming others. This assumption is often thought to be an expression of autonomy interpreted in terms of Mill's 'harm principle' (which we shall shortly discuss). It will emerge that the second assumption can also be challenged.

It might be thought that there is no difficulty about the relationship between autonomy and the pursuit of health within the life or
activities of one person. If people pursue health, this is not an
impairment or diminution of their autonomy but an expression of it.
But can people exercise their autonomy at the *expense* of their own
health? If 'exercising autonomy' were simply a matter of doing
whatever one wanted, and if health were not a value, then this would
be logically possible. But it will be remembered that we have argued
that the autonomous person is not simply self-determining but also
self-governing, where to be 'self-governing' means to be able to
guide one's own conduct in terms of values. Moreover, we have also
argued in the previous section of this chapter that health is a value.
If follows that if a person knowingly pursues a lifestyle which is
destructive of his or her health this cannot count as an expression of
autonomy, unless other values are involved. This qualification must
be added because, as we have previously claimed, a person may
knowingly pursue a course of action which will destroy his or her
own health, but do so in the service of others. For example, someone
may volunteer for service in an unhealthy part of the world, thus
endangering personal health for another worthwhile value. Our
view is that health is *a* value, not that it is the supreme value. But
since it is *a* value it always ought to be one regulator of autonomous
behaviour.

More typical problems arise when we note that A's exercise of
autonomy may affect B's pursuit of health. The classical liberal
solution to this problem is in terms of the 'harm principle'; that A's
right to exercise his or her autonomy should be limited if but only if
he or she is harming B's interests, which in this context is B's health.
This is the liberal idea of freedom, 'negative freedom' or freedom
from external interference provided one is not harming others. The
formulation of this position which is typically quoted here is that of
J.S. Mill (*ibid*; Chapter 1):

the sole end for which mankind are warranted, individually or collectively,
in interfering with the liberty of action of any of their number, is self-
protection . . . His own good, either physical or moral, is not a sufficient
warrant.

If we place this liberal principle in the context of health promotion it
both gives warrant for the most obvious sorts of health legislation,
and also sets limits to paternalistic health care intervention for the
patient's 'own good'.

To begin with the second point, the liberal principle is claiming that no doctor or health legislation can justifiably seek to compel people to take steps to protect or improve their health. This liberal right is safeguarded in many ways. For example, people may discharge themselves from hospital, and they must sign a form consenting to an operation, and so on; but of course this right is confined to aspects of their autonomy which affect only their own interests, and, as we shall see, it is a right which does not really extend very far, even within a liberal framework. This takes us back to the first point—the liberal warrant for health legislation.

First of all, and obviously, a person's right to exercise autonomy may be legitimately curtailed by health legislation when he or she is suffering from certain sorts of infectious disease or mental illness such that the interests or health of others are liable to be harmed. There is no difficulty about the acceptance of this restriction in general terms. The problems arise over the more detailed application of it. For example, a topical question concerns the nature and extent of the restrictions which should be placed on sufferers from AIDS, or the extent of justifiable investigation or reporting of those who may be HIV-positive. Again, it is controversial how far those who are mentally ill should be detained against their will, or what sort of treatment they should have if they are detained.

Pressure for legislation is generated as more becomes known about how diseases are transmitted. For example, the dangers of 'passive smoking' are now appreciated, and other sorts of environmental pollution are now known to cause disease. There is therefore a case for curbing the freedom of both individuals and corporate bodies, such as industries, in the name of the autonomy of other individuals. This issue is, of course, a source of much political debate. Some countries, such as Norway, have banned smoking in many public places, and various 'watch-dogs' keep a close eye on the consequences of the operation of the nuclear industry. But, although there can be political debate about applications of the 'preventing harm to others' idea, the general principle is clear and acceptable.

A second issue concerning the way in which a lack of attention to health may affect the autonomy of others turns on the premise that the vast majority of people play some part in the divisions of labour and make a contribution to society. In other words, it is true, and indeed necessarily true, that citizens have social duties; and most people are citizens. But if we fail to perform our social duties, then either someone else has to perform them for us, or other people are in some way harmed or inconvenienced. Either way involves a lessening of some persons' autonomy. But we cannot perform our social duties adequately or at all without health. The liberal principle therefore justifies, if not health legislation to force us to be healthy, at least the claim that there are *moral* duties to others to maintain our own health.

A third argument which can be used to justify limiting our autonomy in the interests of the pursuit of health is that health care, under any system, is a scarce resource. Health care used by one person is therefore at the expense of health care available for others.

The argument of this section has been that within a liberal framework there is a right but no duty to pursue our own health, unless by not pursuing our own health we are harming others. We draw attention to the limited extent of the freedom that even this liberal view gives us, because of the way in which we affect each other's interests in society. But in any case we have rejected the liberal position on this and have claimed that health is a value in its own right, and that to be autonomous is to be not just self-determining or entitled to do what we might want, but also self-governing and obliged to regulate our conduct by values, including health. To say this, however, is just to say that there is a *moral* duty to pursue our own health. Does a *government* via health legislation, education, and health campaigns have a duty to safeguard or enhance our health other than to prevent harm? To ask this question is to invite discussion of assumptions 3–5 of the liberal position listed in Section 10.2.

10.5 Government interventions

Has the State any justification for using fiscal policy to promote health, or for passing legislation to promote positive health? This is certainly recommended, as we have seen, by principle 3 of the WHO document quoted on p. 141. But the objection might be that positive health is an *ideal* of the good life rather than a *necessity*, and the State has no duty to promote specific ideals of the good life. This follows from the third assumption of the liberal position listed in Section 10.2.

This objection might be rebutted on the grounds that there is a causal link between the negative sense of health (not being ill) and

positive health, such that if the promotion of the conditions conducive to better health in this negative sense can be justified (as it
can on any reasonable political theory), then a justification for the
promotion of positive health can be found on the same basis. The
claim is that the promotion of positive health will bring about
physical and mental health states which are resistant or more resistant to disease agents. A claim of this sort would need a great deal
of empirical evidence to support it, and in any case is always in
danger of being made true by definition—if you do succumb to ill-
health then you did not have enough positive health. Nevertheless,
at a common sense level it seems obviously true that if you are in
general terms fit, then you are less likely to succumb to disease; and
if you do succumb to disease, then you will recover more quickly if
you enjoy 'positive health'. If, therefore, there is justification for
the promotion of health in the negative sense, the same justification
holds for the promotion of positive health.

It might be said that this argument depends on an empirical premise—the so-called 'law of disease'—which is hard to establish,
however plausible it seems to common sense. It would therefore be
preferable if there were some way of arguing that the government
does have a duty to promote health in the positive sense as an ideal of
the good life.

A stronger and simpler way of arguing that a government does
have a duty to promote positive health is to refer to the preamble to
the Constitution of WHO (1946), which asserts that there is a right
to positive health. In ambitious terms it states: 'The enjoyment of
the highest attainable standard of health is one of the fundamental
rights of every human being without distinction of race, religion,
political belief, economic or social condition.' If this is a fundamental right then presumably there is a correlative duty laid upon governments to implement it. In other words, acceptance of the WHO
Constitution commits States to health and welfare policies. How far
such policies can be implemented no doubt turns on the wealth of
the country, but there can be no doubt that wealthy Western nations
are committed to implementing fiscal and legislative policies to
enhance positive health. In our next chapter on 'Social Justice' we
shall look in more detail at the limits and limitations of State intervention in this area.

To argue that there is a duty on governments to promote health
for its own sake still leaves some questions unanswered. Supposing
there is such a duty, can it be implemented other than at the expense

of individual autonomy? To discuss this question is to examine assumptions 4 and 5 of the liberal position listed in Section 10.2: that health legislation necessarily removes autonomy and that autonomy is simply the absence of constraint.

It is easy to slip into the error of regarding all legislation on the model of the criminal law—as restrictive prohibition backed by sanction. But this is an oversimplified way of looking at some health legislation. For example, legislation may require public bodies to make provision for the disabled. This is more aptly seen as a positive creation of new opportunities than as negative prohibition. Again, there are legal requirements on factory owners to restrict unpleasant pollutants, and on car manufacturers to ensure certain safety standards. Indeed, there is an enormous range of health legislation with a positive slant, and whereas this may diminish the freedom of some groups in society, it certainly extends the freedom of the majority and improves their quality of life.

This now takes us to the fifth assumption of the liberal position, an assumption about the nature of autonomy itself. Is autonomy just the absence of constraint? There is no simple way of answering this question. Any attempt to say 'such and such is the central idea of autonomy' is likely to do violence to some important aspect of it. It is possible, however, to distinguish at least one positive aspect to the concept. Just as we distinguished a negative side to health as the absence of disease, and a positive side embracing well-being, so it is possible to distinguish a negative side to autonomy as the absence of constraint, and a positive side as 'being empowered' or as 'self-determination'.

If we think of autonomy in this way then health legislation is not *removing* our individual autonomy but rather *enhancing* it. In improving the general quality of life, legislation can add to our autonomy. This is obviously the case if we consider the example of provision for the disabled, but it is true also of anti-pollution legislation, and many other types of health legislation.

We shall, in conclusion, pull together the main threads of the argument. We have been addressing two main questions: what is the relationship between the pursuit of health and the exercise of autonomy; and what ought to be the position of a government on the pursuit of health by its subjects? In discussing these questions we have considered the liberal framework of thinking on health autonomy and politics, and the ways in which the ideas of health promotion modify that framework.

Taking the first question, we noted that, in terms of liberal assumptions, individuals may exercise their autonomy in the pursuit of health but are not obliged to do so because health is seen as an instrumental value enabling its possessor to obtain a wide range of other goods. Health is thereby simply a causal factor in the pursuit of the good life or, at best, what we have termed a 'liking value'. From the health promotion point of view, however, health is not just an external instrumental means to the exercise of autonomy but an internal component means. Positive health is not just a necessary condition of self-realization but is an actual realization of the self. This last point is difficult and needs some further explanation.

The liberal, we said, sees health as an instrumental means to realizing other sorts of value, but does not see it as itself a value. In the same way, the scaffolding, lorries, cement mixers, building tools, etc. are external instrumental means to the building of a house, and they have no value in their own right. But the bricks, glass, wood, and slates are internal component means to the house; they are part of the finished product. In a similar way, we are claiming that positive health is not just an external instrumental means to the good life for human beings; it is a component value, a part of the good life.

Turning now to the question of how far the government is obliged or justified in using fiscal policy and health legislation to further the positive health of individuals and enhance their autonomy, we argued that if there is a causal link between furthering positive health and preventing ill-health, then there is a duty on governments to further the positive health of individuals as a means of preventing ill-health. More strongly we argued that to the extent that governments accept the WHO Constitution, which states that there is a right possessed by individuals to the best possible health, there is a correlative duty on governments to do what they can to improve health.

Two important qualifications should be noted about this justification. The first is that it does not follow from the fact that there is a human right to health and a correlative duty on governments to do what they can to improve health that there is not also a moral duty on people to do what they can to improve their own health. The parallel is with education. Governments have a duty to create facilities for education, but people have a duty to make the best use of these facilities.

The second qualification is that the duty of a government to improve the health status of its citizens cannot be separated from the duties of social justice. Many studies have shown that the major threats to health in this country are not evenly distributed across the population but are heavily concentrated in the lower social classes. The main thrust of health promotion should therefore be in this area, and again there are parallels with education. It is to the problem of social justice that we shall next turn. The discussion of this problem will also enable us to examine the final assumption of the liberal position—that 'society' is just a fiction to refer to assemblages of individuals and their individual responsibilities.

10.6 Conclusions

1. Health promotion is strongly normative; it endeavours to persuade people to adopt certain lifestyles, and is committed to furthering certain values.

2. The prevailing assumptions of Western society are those of liberalism, and health promotion (which arises from certain new currents of thought) leads to the modification or even rejection of certain of these assumptions.

3. In particular, health promotion sees health not just as an instrumental and 'liking' value (although it is these) but also as an ideal or moral value, something to be approved of for its own sake.

4. Since to be autonomous is not just to be self-determining or free to do what one wants, but also to be self-governing or subject to values, people have a moral duty to pursue health for its own sake, as a value, and not just to prevent harm to others (although even that considerably limits their freedom).

5. But in pursuing health in the fullest sense for its own sake people are expressing their autonomy, their true selves.

6. The government has a duty via health legislation, fiscal policy, and other means to enhance the positive health of individuals since this follows from the WHO claim that there is a human right to health in the fullest sense.

7. Health legislation and fiscal policy do not diminish autonomy but enhance it.

11 Justice, health, and society

It is not immediately clear that questions of social justice are raised by health and its distribution, as distinct from health care, health determinants, and their distribution. Moreover, even if we suppose that questions of social justice do arise over health, we must not immediately conclude that it is entirely the fault of a government if there is social injustice, or even that social injustice in health, if it exists, can always be rectified by government intervention. The relationships between these ideas of health, health care, health determinants, and social justice are of importance to health promotion, since a clarification will help to clarify the political stance of health promotion. Our argument will be that the political stance of health promotion derives from its own professional concerns.

11.1 Health, health care, and health determinants

Is health not just a brute fact about people? For example, it is just a brute fact that some people have the natural capacity to run faster than others, or have better brains than others, or are more attractive than others. This may be unfortunate, but it is not a question of justice, unless we think that God has been unfair. So why is the same not true of health? It might, of course, be said that people have a certain room for choice in respect of their natural capacities—they can improve or neglect their natural capacities and might be praised or blamed for so doing. And again the same is true of health; people can to a limited extent take steps which improve or destroy their health and we might praise or blame them. But these considerations, even if they bring health within the sphere of morality (see Section 10.4), do not make it a matter of social justice. So is health a matter of social justice, or is it just misleading to think of it in those terms.

It might be said that at least *health care* is a matter of social justice. For example, if it could be shown that for no good reason the distribution of GPs, hospitals, and ancillary services was

157

uneven, then this fact would be a legitimate cause of complaint to a government. Even this point assumes, what some liberal purists would deny, that it is the duty of a government, as distinct from the market, to concern itself with the distribution of health care. But despite this qualification there is obviously a case for discussing the distribution of health care in the language of justice.

Moreover, *health determinants* also seem to lie within the field of social justice. By 'health determinants' we mean all those factors, such as housing, diet, leisure facilities, which influence health status. Once again, some theorists might argue that those commodities are market-related and do not directly raise questions of social justice. But most Western governments have diluted the purity of marked-based liberalism with welfarist ideas, and insofar as governments, local or national, provide or regulate the supply of such health determinants, then they may be discussed in the language of social justice.

So far, then, we have distinguished health, health care, and health determinants, and have maintained that, whereas health falls only marginally within the sphere of social justice, health care and health determinants are largely matters of social justice (the extent depending on the extent to which the purity of marked-based liberalism is diluted with welfarist elements).

Unfortunately, however, this account of the relationship between these concepts is too simple. According to the models of health and health promotion recommended in this book the concepts of health, health care, and health determinants are closely connected, and therefore the connection of each with justice is closer than emerges on our account so far, as we shall now show.

First, there is an obvious link between health and health care, in that where the health of a given population compares poorly with that of a wider population there is a *prima facie* case for investigating the adequacy of the health care provided. Secondly, there is also a close causal link between health determinants and individual health, in that such matters as damp housing are obviously factors in producing poor health states in individuals. Indeed, that is why they are called 'health determinants'. This point suggests that, thirdly, and more controversially, the link between health and health determinants is also *conceptual*: health is not just a property of individuals but of social relationships and social structures. This claim requires some expansion.

We have argued that persons are essentially social; it is their nature to be citizens (Section 9.5). Their positive health is therefore continuous with the quality of their social relationships and structures. This is implicit in the W H O definition of health from which we began in Chapter 2. But 'social relationships' and 'social structures' are simply grand terms for what are normally regarded as health determinants—housing, employment, leisure and cultural facilities. In other words, the distinction between health and health determinants is by no means clear-cut, and we can speak of health as being experienced through social relationships. Indeed, we speak quite naturally, and not metaphorically, when we say that the atmosphere in a school, or even more generally in a community, is one of well-being. Perhaps this point is most dramatically made in the example of a well-run and humanely administered hospice. We can say of it that well-being pervades its atmosphere—it enables its inmates to live until they die—regardless of the fact that its inmates, from the point of view of negative health, are terminally ill. In such an institution the social relationships and social structures can properly be said to express well-being (see Section 2.3).

Fourthly, the connection between health care and health determinants is not sharp. Thus, it is by no means clear whether such matters as the provision of community centres for the elderly, or equipment, toilet facilities, and accessible buildings for the disabled, are health care or health determinants. And what of meals-on-wheels, nursery facilities, rehabilitation centres for alcoholics or for mentally disturbed people?

If, then, it is possible to maintain that there are these close connections between health, health care, and health determinants, and if it is plausible to maintain that the latter two raise questions of social justice, then we can also maintain that health itself raises questions of social justice. It does not, of course, follow that it is the fault of the government if a society is unhealthy and unjust. It is common but superficial to heap all the blame for social injustice on the government of the day, and we shall discuss the role of government intervention in Sections 11.3 and 11.4. But the immediate requirement for the argument is to analyse the concept of social justice as it affects health, health care, and health determinants.

11.2 Social justice

The discussion of social justice in health care is often put in the language of equality and we shall discuss it in that language. The very general ideal behind the National Health Service, and other systems that have similar ideals, is that each person has a right to *equal consideration* in respect of health care and that it is the duty of the State to observe that right.

This notion of 'equal consideration', however, needs considerably more examination (Downie and Telfer 1980). In some contexts the demand for equal consideration is merely a demand for consistent treatment as between one person and another: in other words, a demand that people be treated in accordance with some rule which can be formulated. This demand for consistency seems to clash with the more personalized aspects of case-work or patient care, which stress the impossibility of general rules and the uniqueness of the individual situation. But where benefits are being distributed, clients and patients are keen to demand consistency ('Why won't you give to me what you gave to him?') and regard as unfair any difference of this kind which seems to be an arbitrary exception. Consistency is an important aspect of social justice in the context of discussion of the distribution of ill-health among different social classes and geographical areas. Consistency, then, is necessary if distribution of benefit (and, of course, health education, medical treatment, and social work services are themselves benefits) is to be seen as fair.

But consistency alone is not sufficient for fairness. A principle of distribution which could be applied consistently, such as 'Never spend time on an alcoholic', might itself be unfair. To get nearer to the moral principle of equal consideration, we need to find some way of ruling out such possibilities.

What is required is that all differences of treatment be based on a criterion which group like cases together, and distinguish unlike cases, for morally appropriate reasons. In this context the obvious criterion is *need*. Since the aim of proffering help is to meet needs, those whose need is greatest should get more help than those whose need is less, and those whose need is equal should get equal help. This principle, of justified differences in treatment based on the criterion of differing degrees of need, is neatly illustrated by those benefits which are scaled according to the size of the family which is to receive them, or by the provision of more repeat consultations to people of lower social classes to compensate for lack of coping skills (Whitehead 1987).

We shall call this requirement, that any differences of treatment be based on morally appropriate reasons, a principle of equity. Equity is not the same as consistency since it says not only that like cases must be treated equally but also that unlike cases must be treated unequally. In other words, equity can be expressed in 'positive discrimination' (see Section 4.5). As we have seen, equity presupposes a criterion for justifiable differences in the way people are treated. In the context of health this will normally be need. Of course, in other contexts, such as education, other criteria might be relevant, such as capacity, but we shall stick to the health context and the criterion based on need.

So far, then, we have looked at two senses of the right to equal consideration which makes up the concept of social justice in a health context. These were consistency of treatment, a principle which is necessary but not sufficient for social justice in health care, and equity—equality of treatment based on need. Are these concepts sufficient to express our intuitions of social justice?

Perhaps, but some thinkers would have reservations about the adequacy of equity on the grounds that it is both *derivative*, in that it depends on another value, such as need or capacity, before it comes into operation; and *relative*, in that it involves equality only with others in the same group, not with everyone. There is, however, a third approach to 'equal consideration' which we may call *egalitarian equality*. The third sense seems to be neither derivative nor relative; it advocates that all people be treated equally for equality's sake, not just in the course of pursuing other values. A principle of egalitarian equality entails not only trying, when serving people's needs, to do so in an equitable manner, but also redistributing benefits simply to make people more equal when need is not in question. In practice, of course, this distinction between equity and egalitarianism is not clear-cut. What one group sees as organizing taxation and benefits in an equitable way proportionate to the needs of all concerned, another group sees as 'the egalitarian politics of envy'. Again, what can be construed in a given society as needed depends in part on an egalitarian consideration, viz., what other people have: in a society where most people have television, a mains water supply is not a luxury but a need. This point is made in the *Black Report* (1980; p. 107) as follows:

Poverty is also a relative concept, and those who are unable to share the amenities or facilities provided within a rich society, or who are unable to fulfil the social and occupational obligations placed upon them by virtue of their limited resources, can properly be regarded as poor. They may also be relatively disadvantaged in relation to the risks of illness or accident or the factors positively promoting health.

The spirit of egalitarian equality is important for the present argument, since it lies behind the *Black Report* and many discussions of social justice in the context of health, health care, and health determinants.

We spoke just now of the egalitarians' aim to 'make people more equal'. But the question immediately arises—equal in what respect? For it is possible to draw a broad contrast between the ideal of equality in respect of opportunity—equality in the starting and running conditions of the race of life—and equality in respect of outcome—the ideal of proceeding side by side throughout the race to a 'tie' at the finish. It is fairly common for those of moderate opinion to commit themselves to the first of these ideals rather than the second. But the second also is aimed at by many social thinkers at the present time. Moreover, the truth may be (although believers in equality of opportunity have not always faced up to it) that the first cannot be secured in independence of the second. For even if you provide equality of opportunity, then, granted the truth of some uncontroversial propositions about the variation in human ability, industry, etc., the tendency will be towards inequality of outcome or satisfaction. Perhaps, then, we must say that if the welfare services are really concerned with equality as an ideal, they are concerned to secure not just 'equal opportunities' but 'equal outcomes'. In other words, there is commitment to positive discrimination. This seems to be the view of the *Black Report*.

To bring this out, consider an argument in the *Black Report* concerned with equality of opportunity of access to GP consultations. They point out that for most years covered by the General Household Survey the number of people consulting a doctor, and the average number of consultations, has tended to increase with descending social class. In other words, the figures seem to suggest that, for curative if not preventive services, there is equality of opportunity to use the services. But the *Black Report* (p. 69) does not draw this conclusion. The authors say: 'This may partially miss the point. It may be that the proper basis for comparing rates of consultation is not one of simple population but of the *need* for care'. In other words, they conclude that the greater consultation rates suggest a greater need for care which is not being satisfied. The preferred ideal is therefore thought to be equality of outcome or satisfaction, and not just equality of opportunity.

The same point is made by Whitehead (1987; p. 271). One study cited suggested that doctors gave more repeat consultations to lower social class patients to compensate for their lack of coping skills. This suggests equality of opportunity. Another study took the same data to suggest that 'the lower occupational classes had more illness which was life-threatening and more painful in nature than higher classes'. In other words, the second writer did not see equality of outcome because there is lack of equality of need.

So far we have considered three applications of the moral idea of equality of consideration: the equality of consistency; the relative equality of equity which derives from need; egalitarian equality which is neither derivative nor relative.

All three notions of equality, however, presuppose a fourth more fundamental kind of equality in terms of which it is assumed that all human beings ought to be regarded as equal. Egalitarian equality assumes that *all* human beings ought to have equal satisfactions, and does not exclude any group from its scope. Equity, although it does not say that everyone should be treated equally, incorporates the demand that differences in treatment must be *morally justified*: in other words, the presumption is that people should be treated equally *unless* there is moral warrant for treating them differently. Both principles therefore rule out the option of leaving some group out of one's moral calculations altogether. Thus, respect for equity precludes us from saying 'Don't bother about the mentally handicapped' for instance.

But if the underlying concept is supposed to involve the notion that there is a respect in which people *are* equal, as a matter of fact, it is clearly mistaken. People are manifestly *unequal* in physique, in mental capacity, in physical attractiveness, in moral goodness, in any respect that can be thought of. We do however speak of people as of equal *worth* or *value*. Given that people are *not* in fact equal, can any sense be made of this idea?

The notion of human beings as of equal worth makes sense if it is regarded, not as a statement of fact about human beings, but as a principle prescribing how they are to be treated. But the importance of the principle does not lie in its stress on *equality*, but in its stress on human worth. The point is that each individual human being is to be treated as having worth or value in him or herself. Human beings do not have a price—they are not replaceable by anything else, even by other human beings—they individually have what Kant calls *dignity*, the value of something which is irreplaceable. This is again the principle of respect for the individual which we have already introduced (Section 9.6), and it carries with it the idea that no one's claims may be ignored, however great the gain to others, because a price cannot be put on any individual's welfare. This point can be put in terms of equality by saying that everyone is of equal importance, but the equality is after all *derivative*, in the sense that it depends on another moral value, that of respect for the individual. We can depict consistency, equity, and egalitarian equality as manifestations of respect for the individual, deployed in a social context; all three, but particularly egalitarian equality, are also called social justice, and all three are constitutive of societal well-being, or a flourishing society.

11.3 Explaining the health divide

The preceding discussion of the complex idea of equality has brought out that whether we stress consistency, equity, or egalitarian equality, large inequalities in health status are morally unjustifiable. Does the fact that there are wide differences in health status among social classes therefore constitute an *injustice*? The answer here depends on the explanation of the health inequalities between the social classes. The *Black Report* (1980) and its sequel *The Health Divide* (Whitehead 1987) offer four possible explanations of the differentials. The first of these is what they call the 'artefact' explanation—that the method of measuring occupational class artificially inflates the size and importance of health differences. This is rightly dismissed on the grounds, among others, that on any index of social circumstances the findings are more or less consistent with those based on occupational class gradients.

The second explanation is in terms of natural and social selection. People in poor health slide down the occupational and social scales. There is something in this but the evidence suggests that it accounts for only a small proportion of the health differential between social classes.

The third explanation, the structuralist—materialist explanation, stresses the conditions and pressures of the environment—poor housing, dangerous work, fewer resources—which lead to poor health states.

The fourth explanation stresses cultural—behavioural differences; lower social classes adopt a more dangerous and health-damaging life style than higher social classes, as a result of a 'culture of poverty' or 'transmitted deprivation'.

Clearly, the most plausible explanations, which are all elaborated with sophistication in the *Black Report* and the *Health Divide*, are the third and fourth, and each of them appeals to a different set of values. The fourth explanation stresses individual moral responsibility for health states. It might be said that nobody can now be ignorant of the dangers of cigarette smoking or of a high-fat diet. If, therefore, people persist in both, their consequential ill-health is their own fault. By contrast, the third explanation depicts behaviour as determined by social and economic conditions. A good example of the differences in approach is in the rival explanations of childhood accidents (Whitehead 1987; p. 62).

The observation that children from lower social groups have more accidents than children from higher groups may be explained by the behavioural view as due to more reckless risk-taking behaviour in this group and inadequate care by parents. The materialist view would highlight the unsafe play areas, the lack of fenced-off gardens, and the greater difficulty of supervising children's play from high-rise housing. In the latter view the environment is dictating the behaviour of both mother and child.

What bearing do these rival explanations have on the question of whether the health divide constitutes a social injustice? If the fourth explanation is stressed, then it is arguable that the health divide is not mainly a matter of social injustice. There may be some social injustice if it can be shown that people belonging to lower social classes are not adequately informed, or that health care, housing, and leisure facilities are sub-standard. But basically this approach emphasizes individual responsibility for poor health in lower social classes. Many writers on health promotion use the term 'victim blaming' to describe this emphasis (see p. 31), and no doubt it is sometimes no more than that.

But, as we shall see, there is also an important and valid point to be made through this approach: health cannot be achieved through any 'top-down' services or hand-outs, but only via a 'bottom-up' approach. Any other view is basically patronizing to the people involved. Autonomy, of course, as we have already stressed, is something to be *achieved*, rather than something which people possess regardless of their social and economic conditions, and it is this that the third explanation emphasizes; the term 'empowerment' brings this out. Hence, as we have stressed, many writers on health promotion prefer to use that term rather than 'autonomy'.

Does it then constitute a social injustice that health determinants, the social and economic conditions for health, are much poorer in some than in other areas of society? It may do, but no one should underestimate the consequences, economic and political, of attempting to remedy this state of affairs. When the *Black Report* was published in 1980 the Secretary of State for Social Services pointed out in a Foreword that the additional expenditure involved in endorsing the recommendations was upward of 2 billion pounds sterling per year at 1980 prices. He therefore did not endorse the recommendations. Now it is easy to blame governments for failing to improve social conditions, and the evidence is that the health divide has increased since 1980. But in a democratic society a government can do only what its electorate shows a political will for it to do, and there is no evidence that the electorate is willing to countenance the massive redistribution of resources which would be involved in an additional expenditure of that magnitude. To say this is not to say that much more cannot be done by governments even within this democratic mandate.

Indeed, even in terms of a liberal view, a government can still be pressed to do a great deal towards creating a healthy environment, insisting on regulations for industrial waste, the minimizing of pollution, and so on. The argument is that even on a negative conception of government there would be a requirement to protect citizens from disease, and no clear line can be drawn between this and the positive furthering of the health of the inhabitants by public health legislation. It is important to stress this because it is common to despise *laissez-faire* political philosophy on the grounds, among others, that is has nothing positive to advocate on health care. Yet if it can consistently advocate public health legislation it can, and historically did, achieve as much an improvement in the nation's health as the National Health Service; for an adequate system of sanitation and other population health protection measures have done more for the health of the nation than any subsequent improvements in medical services, including the present high-cost technological medicine. But there is no political will in Western democracies for the massive redistribution entailed by the *Black Report*.

Let us turn from health determinants to the provision of health care facilities and services for individuals. The question is whether they can be categorized, in liberal terms, in the same way as population health measures. In other words, can the provision of health care by the State be seen as the provision of a commodity which is under-supplied in market terms and one which therefore makes a claim on a liberal government?

On a pure version of the liberal or *laissez-faire* theory of the State, health services would not count as what economists call 'joint' or 'non-excludable' or 'under-supplied' in market terms. They would not therefore call for government action, and therefore inequality in the distribution of those goods would not constitute a social injustice, as distinct from an individual failing to ensure adequate health insurance. But most countries in the West, apart perhaps from the USA, do not have pure versions of liberal individualism, and in diluted forms of liberalism the state provision of health care does not seem anomalous.

Now, if the state does provide health care it can reasonably be criticized for any wide differences in the distribution of health care, and this will be a criticism in the language of social justice. It is a matter for complex factual investigation, such as is exemplified in the *Black Report* and the *Health Divide*, whether any given countries can be criticized for this at any given period. We shall not dwell on this, important though it is, because many studies have dealt with it. It is sufficient for us to note the conclusion that on all except pure versions of the liberal state the distribution of health care facilities does raise a question of social justice.

We wish to lay stress on another aspect of the matter. This aspect is still in a sense political, but it raises practical issues which can be taken up by the health promotion movement.

11.4 Community and citizenship

Let us begin by asking the question: 'Suppose a government were to endorse the recommendations of the *Black Report*, would they bring about health for all?' The answer is 'no', because no amount of improvement in social conditions is a substitute for people themselves taking responsibility for their own health and their own neighbourhood. This is the truth in the cultural/behavioural explanations of the health divide in the *Black Report* and the *Health Divide*. On the other hand, it is entirely unrealistic to expect individuals on their own, in deprived areas or circumstances, to take full responsibility for their own health and well-being. Assistance, advice, and leadership are required, and it is precisely this that the health promotion movement is about, and it is from this purely professional concern that the distinctive health promotion concept of 'empowerment' derives.

The provision of professional help in community development (see p. 42) is best carried out on a multi-disciplinary basis. For example, health education/promotion officers must work along with social work services, local churches, and the general public. The danger to be avoided is the one into which the delivery of health care has fallen. The delivery of health care has often been criticized for using 'top-down' methods and over-emphasizing 'magic bullets', which are wrongly thought by the public to be capable of curing every ailment known to human beings. This criticism, which has been given its most trenchant formulation by Ivan Illich (1977), is that health care workers, and the whole context of health care, have become what we might term 'over-professionalized'. The impression has been conveyed over several decades that an ordinary person cannot really manage his or her own health and welfare, and that for any of the ills of life there is an expert who will help.

There are three connected aspects of this criticism (Downie and Telfer 1980). The first is what we might call the medicalization of ordinary experience. In other words, we have all been encouraged to think that every human anxiety, discomfort, or misery is a medical or related problem. Where in the past people might have thought that sleeplessness is something that you can treat yourself, that anxiety or grief are to be shared with a clergyman, a friend, or a neighbour, or that discomforts or miseries are to be put up with until they go away, we now turn to the doctor for a pill.

Going along with the medicalization of experience there is, secondly, the complementary belief that for every ailment there is an expert to help. Those in the health care business have not discouraged either of these beliefs and have warned of the dangers of not consulting the doctor in time, of not contacting welfare services, of not having regular checks on one's teeth, and so on; and now specialist health promoters have emerged as a new generation of experts dominating the media with the high-pressure selling of positive health.

The outcome of this takes us to the third and most important point for present purposes. The medicalization of ordinary experience plus the rise of the expert has had the result that people have lost confidence in their own abilities to take responsibility for their own health in particular and their own lives in general. Ordinary people have come to feel that they do not have the expertise needed to help with family or similar difficulties. As a consequence many people have lost the feeling that there is a moral need to have any concern for one's neighbour; 'they' can now be relied on to do everything. All three criticisms point in the same direction: the delivery of health care has had a tendency to sap individual freedom, positively conceived, by removing our sense that we are in control of our own health.

The cure for all these ills is the same. Those involved in health care and health promotion must abandon their professional isolation and begin to work *through* the community rather than *on* it, in order to do things *with* the community rather than *to* it. To be fair, there are many signs that this has begun to happen and the health promotion movement can take some credit for the greater stress on *community* involvement in health. There has, in fact, been a growth in recent years of self-help groups—from the familiar Alcoholics Anonymous groups to the many types of parents' groups concerned with education, bereavement, and every sort of serious childhood disease. The growth of such self-help movements should be encouraged and informed by those in professional health care. One of the five principles identified by WHO (1984) is that 'health promotion aims particularly at effective and concrete public participation.'

Indeed, for adequate health care, for the reduction of negative health and the promotion of positive health, we require not just that we should be served by authorized representatives with the rights, duties, skills, and values of the health care professions; not just that these representatives should co-operate in teams for our total health; for wholeness or well-being we require that we should all see ourselves as members of a collectively responsible society. In other words, the members of the health care professions must be assisted by our own striving to become (in the words of St Paul) members one of another. This view of society depicts it as a community with a communal good not entirely reducible to the individual goods of the persons who make it up. In other words, it is a view of society which is importantly different from the liberal view. It is one alternative to the final liberal assumption (see list in Section 10.2) that 'society' is just a convenient fiction to refer to the individuals who occupy a given area at a given time. To put it another way, if society is just individuals then these individuals are *citizens*, or individuals with social responsibilities and a social well-being. This is one implication of the theory of health education we developed in Section 3.4.

To the extent that there is exclusive emphasis on the *State* delivery of health care to individuals, there is the invitation to see health as a commodity to be supplied by the State. The same is true if we think of health as a commodity bought by private health insurance. But health is not in any sense a commodity. Health and well-being are in the end a set of relationships among citizens. As Beauchamp (1987; p. 72) put it:

Collective goods are ultimately a set of relationships among the citizens of a community, relationships in which the community as a whole participates to obtain desired benefits. These collective goods include aggregate states of welfare or wellbeing, including declining rates of disease and premature deaths; efforts to limit the resources society devotes to personal health services; shared and common access to a good like medical care to foster the sense of community and membership in the group itself. And finally, there are those highly important collective goods, shared or common beliefs and values.

It is clear that we can add a legal system to Beauchamp's list, and in particular one designed to stimulate social responsibility. Indeed, it is plausible to suggest that the increasing government intervention on drunk-driving issues has encouraged a greater social awareness about the dangers of alcohol more generally, and thus a greater sense of community and individual responsibility. In a similar way, legislation designed to assist disabled or handicapped persons can also increase a sense of community responsibility for those groups. In other words, in so far as health legislation and other govern-mental health policies are directed at increasing community aware-ness, as distinct from being directed at the good of specific individuals, it is not paternalistic.

We shall conclude by putting our point in terms of grammar, as a change from the more usual sociological or medical models of health and health education. Health can be and traditionally was seen as an *adjective*—a kind of attribute or property which individ-uals could possess, which could be protected by vaccination and impaired by disease. According to more recent ways of looking at health, health is an *adverb*—a style of living, a way of qualifying the active verbs of living. This is part of the promotional or lifestyle approach to health. But we want to suggest that health can also be seen as a *relational predicate*—that health, especially positive health or well-being, can be seen as a set of relationships in which the community as a whole participate to obtain mutual benefits, benefits which include a decline in ill-health and the enhancement of well-being through the shared values of citizenship.

11.5 Conclusions

1. We argued that the initially plausible view—that health care and health determinants, but not health itself, are appropriate subjects for judgements of justice—breaks down when the links between all three are noted.

2. Social justice can be understood as (a) consistency in the supply of goods and services to different areas or social classes; (b) equity based on the criterion of need; (c) egalitarianism, or equality for its own sake. Strands (b) and (c) are often confused, and all three presuppose (d) the equality of human worth, which is an expression of the basic principle of respect for the autonomous individual.

3. The difficulties of achieving equity, far less egalitarian equality, are considerable, and although even a market-based government can be expected to show some positive discrimination to affect the balance of social justice, there is no sign that any Western democracy has the political will to make the massive redistribution involved in recommendations such as those of the *Black Report*.

4. In any case, a 'top-down' governmental intervention cannot bring about health for all in the WHO sense of health. What is needed is a new sense of community responsibility or citizenship. The health promotion movement is essential in facilitating this development.

5. It is in the facilitating of the sense of community by all methods that the political stance of health promotion is to be found.

Further reading

Chapter 2

Seedhouse, D. (1986). *Health: the foundations for achievement*. Wiley, Chichester.

Chapter 3

Ewles, L. and Simnett, I. (1985). *Promoting health. A practical guide to health education*. Wiley, Chichester.

Fletcher, C. (1973). *Communication in medicine*. Nuffield Provincial Hospitals Trust, London.

Chapter 4

Ashton, J. and Seymour, H. (1988). *The new public health*. Open University Press, Milton Keynes.

DHSS (Department of Health and Social Security) (1976). *Prevention and health: everybody's business*. HMSO, London.

EARHA (East Anglian Regional Health Authority) (1988). *Health promotion. A new strategy to 1994*. EARHA, Cambridge.

FCM (Faculty of Community Medicine) (1986). *Health for all by the year 2000. Charter for action*. FCM, London.

Gray, J.A.M. and Fowler, G. (1984). *Essentials of preventive medicine*. Blackwell, Oxford.

O'Neill, P. (1983). *Health crisis 2000*. World Health Organization, Copenhagen.

Research Unit in Health and Behavioural Change, University of Edinburgh (1989). *Changing the public health*. Wiley, Chichester.

Smith, A. and Jacobson, B. (ed.) (1988). *The Nation's health. A strategy for the 1990s*. King Edward's Hospital Fund, London.

Tannahill, A. (1987). Regional health promotion planning and monitoring. *Health Education Journal*, **46**, 125–7.

Taylor, P. (1985). *The smoke ring: tobacco, money and multinational politics*. Sphere, London.

Chapter 6

Council of Europe Committee of Ministers (1988). *School health education and the role of training of teachers*. Recommendation No. R (88) 7.

David, K. and Williams, T. (ed.) (1987). *Health education in schools*, (2nd edn). Harper and Row, Cambridge.

Department of Education and Science (1977). *Health education in schools*. HMSO, London.

Gray, J. A. M. and Fowler, G. (1983). *Preventive medicine in general practice*. Oxford University Press.

Chapter 9

Beauchamp, T. L. and Childress, J. F. (1983). *Principles of biomedical ethics*, (2nd edn). Oxford University Press.

Downie, R. S. and Telfer, E. (1980). *Caring and curing*. Methuen, London.

Chapter 10

Doxiadis, S. (ed.) (1987). *Ethical dilemmas in health promotion*. Wiley, Chichester.

Doxiadis, S. (ed.) (1990). *Ethics in health education*. Wiley, Chichester.

Chapter 11

Campbell, A. V. (1976). *Medicine, health and justice*. Churchill Livingstone, Edinburgh.

Plant, R., Lesser, H., and Taylor-Gooby, P. (1980). *Political philosophy and social welfare*. Routledge and Kegan Paul, London.

Vincent, A. and Plant, R. (1984). *Philosophy, politics and citizenship*. Blackwell, Oxford.

References

Alderson, M. (1976). *An introduction to epidemiology*, p. 172. Macmillan, London.

Anonymous (1981). Commentary from Westminster. Blocking of Bill on tobacco advertising. *Lancet*, **1**, 1377-8.

Antonovsky, A. (1984). The sense of coherence as a determinant of health. In *Behavioural health. A handbook of health enhancement and disease prevention*, (ed. J.D. Matarrazzo, S.M. Veiss, A.J. Herd, and N. Miller). Wiley, New York.

Ajzen, I. and Fishbein, M. (1977). Attitude—behaviour relations: a theoretical analysis and review of empirical research. *Psychological Bulletin*, **84**, 888-918.

Arnold, M.F. (1972). Evaluation: a parallel process to planning. In *Administering health systems: issues and perspectives*. (ed. M.F. Arnold, L.V. Blenkenship, and J.M. Hess). Aldine-Atherton, Chicago.

Aronson, E., Turner, J., and Carlsmith, J.M. (1963). Communicator credibility and communication discrepancy. *Journal of Abnormal and Social Psychology*, **67**, 31-6.

ASH (Action on Smoking and Health), BMA (British Medical Association), and HEA (Health Education Authority) (1988). *Two good reasons for a tobacco pricing policy*. ASH/BMA/HEA, London.

Atkinson, A.B. and Townsend, J.L. (1977). Economic aspects of reduced smoking. *Lancet*, **2**, 492-4.

Baric, L. (1980). Evaluation: obstacles and potentialities. *International Journal of Health Education*, **23**, 142-9.

Beauchamp, D. (1987). Life-style, public health and paternalism. In *Ethical dilemmas in health promotion*, (ed. S. Doxiadis). Wiley, Chichester.

Black Report (1980). Published in 1988 as *Inequalities in health*. (ed. P. Townsend, N. Davidson, and M. Whitehead). Penguin, Harmondsworth.

BMA (British Medical Association) (1986). *Smoking out the barons: the campaign against the tobacco industry*. Wiley, Chichester.

Cameron, D. (1985). Warning against US tobacco sachets. *The Scotsman*, 26 July.

Catford, J.C. (1983). Positive health indicators—towards a new information base for health promotion. *Community Medicine*, **5**, 125-32.

Chaiken, S. and Stangor, C. (1987). Attitudes and attitude change. *Annual Review of Psychology*, **38**, 575-630.

Chiang, C. L. (1965). An index of health: mathematical models. *Public Health Service Publ No 1000, Series 2, No. 5*. National Center for Health Statistics, US Government Printing Office, Washington.

Chiang, C. L. and Cohen, R. D. (1973). How to measure health: a stochastic model for an index of health. *International Journal of Epidemiology*, **20**, 7–13.

Chisholm, J. W. (1990). The 1990 contract: its history and its content. *British Medical Journal*, **300**, 853–6.

Dennis, J., *et al.* (1982). Prevention is possible if you try. *The Health Services*, **37**, 13.

DHSS (Department of Health and Social Security) (1985). *Snuff-dipping— 'Skoal Bandits'*. Letter from Chief Medical Officer, CMO (85) 6.

DHSS (Department of Health and Social Security) (1988). *Public health in England*. Report of the Committee of Inquiry into the future development of the public health function (Chairman Sir Donald Acheson). HMSO, London.

Downie, R. S. and Calman, K. C. (1987). *Healthy respect: ethics and health care*. Faber and Faber, London.

Downie, R. S. and Telfer, E. (1980). *Caring and curing*. Methuen, London.

Draper, P., Griffiths, J., Dennis, J., and Popay, J. (1980). Three types of health education. *British Medical Journal*, **281**, 493–5.

Eisenberg, L. (1987). Social policies for promoting health. In *Ethical dilemmas in health promotion* (ed. S. Doxiadis). Wiley, Chichester.

Engleman, S. (1987). The impact of mass media anti-smoking publicity. *Health Promotion*, **2**, 63–74.

Ewles, L. and Simnett, I. (1985). *Promoting health. A practical guide to health education*. Wiley, Chichester.

Everly, G. S., Smith, K. J., and Haight, G. T. (1987). Evaluating health promotion programmes in the workplace: behavioural models versus financial models. *Health Education Research*, **2**, 61–7.

FCM (Faculty of Community Medicine) (1988). *Alcohol. The prevention of problems related to its use*. FCM, London.

Festinger, L. (1957). *A theory of cognitive dissonance*. Standord University Press.

Festinger, L. and Carlsmith, J. M. (1959). Cognitive consequences of forced compliance. *Journal of Abnormal and Social Psychology*, **58**, 203–10.

Forader, A. (1970). Modifying social attitudes toward the physically disabled through three different modes of instruction. *Dissertation Abstracts International*, **30** (9-B), 4360.

Freedman, J. L. and Steinbruner, J. D. (1964). Perceived choice and resistance to persuasion. *Journal of Abnormal and Social Psychology*, **68**, 678–81.

Frey, D. (1986). Recent research on selective exposure to information. In *Advances in Experimental Social Psychology*, Vol. 19, (ed. L. Berkowitz). Academic Press, Orlando.

Fullard, E., Fowler, G., and Gray, M. (1987). Promoting prevention in primary care: controlled trial of low technology, low cost approach. *British Medical Journal*, **294**, 1080–2.

Galtung, J. (1967). *Theory and methods of social research*. Allen and Unwin, London.

Green, L. W. (1977). Evaluation and measurement: some dilemmas for health education. *American Journal of Public Health*, **67**, 155–61.

Green, L. W. and Lewis, F. M. (1987). Data analysis in the evaluation of health education: toward standardization of procedures and terminology. *Health Education Research*, **2**, 215–21.

Green, L. W., Kreuter, M. W., Deeds, S. G., and Partridge, K. B. (1980). *Health education planning: a diagnostic approach*. Mayfield, Palo Alto.

Harrison, D. F. N. (1986). Editorial. Dangers of snuff, both 'wet' and 'dry'. *British Medical Journal*, **293**, 405–6.

Health Education Studies Unit (1982). *Final report of the patient project*. Health Education Council, London.

Heider, F. (1944). Social perception and phenomenal causality. *Psychological Review*, **51**, 358–74.

Heider, F. (1958). *The psychology of interpersonal relations*. Wiley, New York.

Howitt, D. (1982). *The mass media and social problems*. Pergamon, Oxford.

Hovland, C. I. and Janis, I. L. (ed.) (1959). *Personality and persuasibility*. Yale University Press.

Hunt, S. M., McEwen, J., and McKenna, S. P. (1986). *Measuring health status*. Croom Helm, London.

Illich, I. (1977). *Limits to medicine*. Penguin, Harmonsworth.

Kant, I. (1782). *Groundwork of the metaphysics of morals*, (1st edn) (ed. H. J. Paton) (1948). Hutchinson, London.

Kendell, R. E., de Roumanie, M., and Ritson, E. B. (1983). Influence of an increase in excise duty on alcohol consumption and its adverse effects. *British Medical Journal*, **293**, 405–6.

King Edward's Hospital Fund for London (1989). *Blood cholestrol measurement in the prevention of coronary heart disease*. Consensus statement. King's Fund Centre, London.

LaPiere, R. T. (1934). Attitudes versus action. *Social Forces*, **13**, 230–7.

Last, J. M. (ed.) (1988). *A dictionary of epidemiology*, (2nd edn). Oxford University Press.

Lawrence, D. (1981). The development of a self-esteem questionnaire. *British Journal of Educational Psychology*, **51**, 245–51.

Ledwith, F. (1986). Can evaluation be effective or even cost effective? *Health Education Research*, **1**, 295–8.

Ley, P., *et al.* (1976). Improving doctor—patient communication in general practice. *Journal of the Royal College of General Practitioners*, **26**, 720–4.

Likert, R. (1932). *A technique for the measurement of attitudes. Archives of Psychology*, **140**, 44–53.

McConkey, R., McCormack, B., and Naughton, M. (1983). Changing young people's perceptions of mentally handicapped adults. *Journal of Mental Deficiency Research*, **27**, 279–90.

Maccoby, N. and Alexander, J. (1980). Use of media in lifestyle programmes. In *Behavioural medicine: changing health lifestyles*. (ed. P.O. Davidson and S.M. Davidson). Brunner Mazel, New York.

Maccoby, N. and Farquhar, J.W. (1975). Communication for health: unselling heart disease. *Journal of Communication*, **25**, 114–26.

McKeown, T. (1976). *The role of medicine: dream, mirage or nemesis?*, p. 108. Nuffield Provincial Hospitals Trust, London.

Medrich, E.A. (1979). Constant television: a background to daily life. *Journal of Communication*, **29**, 171–6.

Mill, J.S. (1859). *On liberty*, (ed. M. Warnock) (1962). Collins, London.

Mill, J.S. (1861). *Utilitarianism*, (ed. M. Warnock) (1962). Collins, London.

Ministry of Health (1964). *Health education*. Report of the Joint Committee of the Central and Scottish Health Services Councils (Chairman, Lord Cohen of Birkenhead). HMSO, London.

NALGO (National Association of Local Government Officers) (1984). *Health promotion and the grading of health education officers*. NALGO NHS Circular HS 6020, London.

Nutbeam, D. (1986). Health promotion glossary. *Health Promotion*, **1**, 113–27.

OPCS (Office of Population Censuses and Surveys) (1983). *Smoking attitudes and behaviour*. HMSO, London.

Osgood, C.E., Suci, G.J., and Tannenbaum, P.H. (1957). *The measurement of meaning*. University of Illinois Press.

Pinet, G. (1987). Health legislation, prevention and ethics. In *Ethical dilemmas in health promotion*. (ed. S. Doxiadis). Wiley, Chichester.

Ribeaux, S. and Poppleton, S.E. (1978). *Psychology and work—an introduction*. Macmillan, London.

Roberts, J.L. (1986). *Code busting by tobacco companies*. North Western Regional Health Authority, Manchester.

Roberts, J.L. (1987). *More honour'd in the breach . . . how the 1986 voluntary agreement on tobacco advertising is being broken*. Project Smoke Free, Manchester.

Roediger, H.L., Rushton, J.P., Capaldi, E.D., and Paris, S.G. (1984). *Psychology*. Little Brown, Boston.

Russell, M.A.H., Wilson, C., Taylor, C., and Baker, C.D. (1979). Effect of general practitioners' advice against smoking. *British Medical Journal*, **2**, 231–5.

Schools Council (1977*a*). *All about me 5–8*. Nelson, London.

Schools Council (1977*b*). *Think well 9–13*. Nelson, London.

Schools Council (1982). *Health education 13–18*. Forbes, London.

Smith, A. (1987). Qualms about QALYs. *Lancet*, **1**, 1134–6.

Smith, E. A. (1979). In *Health education. Perspectives and choices* (ed. I. Sutherland), p. 93. George Allen and Unwin, London.

Sutton, S. R. and Hallett, R. (1987). Experimental evaluation of the BBC TV series 'So You Want To Stop Smoking?'. *Addictive Behaviours*, **12**, 363–6.

Tannahill, A. (1985*a*). Reclassifying prevention. *Public Health, London*, **99**, 364–6.

Tannahill, A. (1985*b*). What is health promotion? *Health Education Journal*, **44**, 167–8.

Tannahill, A. (1988*a*). Health for all by the year 2000. Promoting health in East Anglia. In *Promoting health in East Anglia*, Conference report. East Anglian Regional Health Authority, Cambridge.

Tannahill, A. (1988*b*). Editorial. *Community Medicine*, **10**, 94–7.

Tannahill, A. (1990). Health education and health promotion: planning for the 1990s. *Health Education Journal*, **49**, 194–8.

Tannahill, A. and Robertson, G. (1986). Health education in medical education: collaboration, not competition. *Medical Teacher*, **8**, 165–70.

Thurstone, L. L. (1928). Attitudes can be measured. *American Journal of Sociology*, **33**, 529–54.

Tones, B. K. (1981). Affective education and health. In *Health education in schools* (ed. J. Cowley, K. David, and T. Williams). Harper and Row: London.

Tones, B. K. (1983). Education and health promotion: new direction. *Journal of the Institute of Health Education*, **21**, 121–31.

US NIH (United States National Institute of Health) (1986). *Health implications of smokeless tobacco*. Consensus development conference statement, Vol. 6, No. 1. NIH, Washington.

Verbrugge, L. M. (1978). Peers as recruiters: family planning communications in West Malaysian acceptors. *Journal of Health and Social Behaviour*, **19**, 51–68.

Vincent, A. and Plant, R. (1984). *Philosophy, politics and citizenship*. Blackwell, Oxford.

Walster, E. and Festinger, L. (1962). The effectiveness of 'overheard' persuasive communications. *Journal of Abnormal and Social Psychology*, **65**, 395–402.

Wallston, K. A. and Wallston, B. S. (1978). Development of the Multidimensional Health Locus of Control (MHLC) scales. *Health Education Monographs*, **6** (2).

Wheldall, K. (1975). *Social behaviour*. Methuen, London.

Whitehead, M. (1987). *The health divide: inequalities in health in the 1980s*. Health Education Council, London.

WHO (World Health Organization) (1946). *Constitution*. WHO, New York.

WHO (World Health Organization) (1984). *Health promotion. A discussion document on the concept and principles.* WHO, Copenhagen.

WHO (World Health Organization) (1985). *Targets for health for all.* WHO, Copenhagen.

WHO (World Health Organization) (1986). *Ottawa Charter for Health Promotion.* WHO.

Williams, A. (1983). The economic role of 'health indicators'. In *Measuring the social benefits of medicine*, (ed. G. Teeling Smith). OHE, London.

Williams, T. (1987). Health education in secondary schools. In *Health education in schools*, (ed. K. David and T. Williams). Harper and Row, London.

Winn, D.M. *et al.* (1981). Snuff dipping and oral cancer among women in the Southern United States. *New England Journal of Medicine*, **304**, 745-9.

Zajonc, R.B. (1968). Attitudinal effects of mere exposure. *Journal of Personality and Social Psychology, Monograph Supplement*, **9** (2), 1-27.

Zimmerman, G.A. (1985). Humor for peace. In *Working for peace*, (ed. N. Wollman). Impact, London.

Index